AUTHENTIC TRANSCRIPTIONS
WITH NOTES AND TABLATURE

THE
BEATLES
THE CAPITOL ALBUMS
VOLUME 2

D0939841

Music transcriptions by Mike Butzen, Jesse Gress,
Bill LaFleur, Andrew Moore and Ron Piccione

ISBN 978-1-4234-2995-1

HAL•LEONARD®
CORPORATION
7777 W. BLUEMOUND RD. P.O. BOX 13819 MILWAUKEE, WI 53213

Visit Hal Leonard Online at
www.halleonard.com

THE EARLY BEATLES

BEATLES IV

from *The Early Beatles*

Love Me Do

Words and Music by John Lennon and Paul McCartney

*Harmonica arr. for gtr.

**Chord symbols reflect basic harmony.

Some - one to love, some - bod - y new. _____

D.S. al Coda 1

Some - one to love, some - one like ___ you.

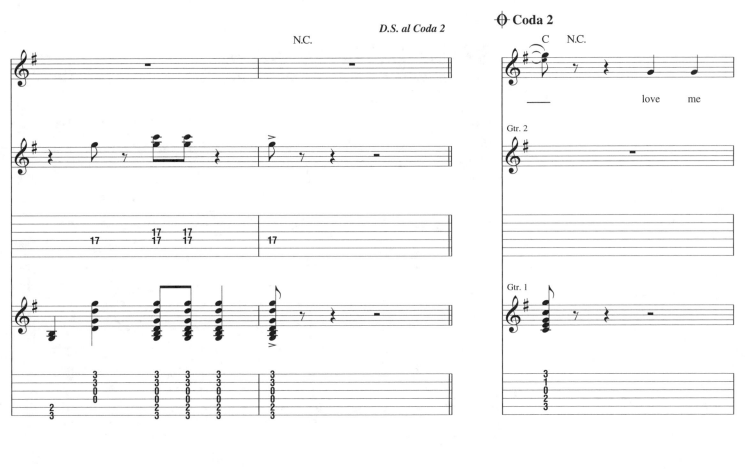

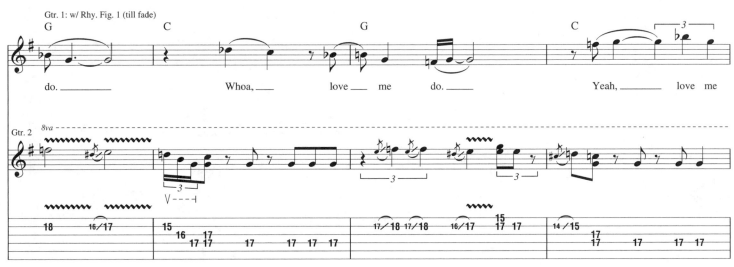

from *The Early Beatles*

Twist and Shout

Words and Music by Bert Russell and Phil Medley

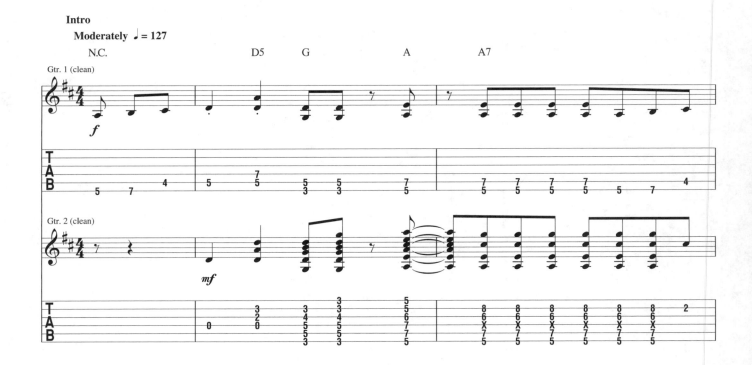

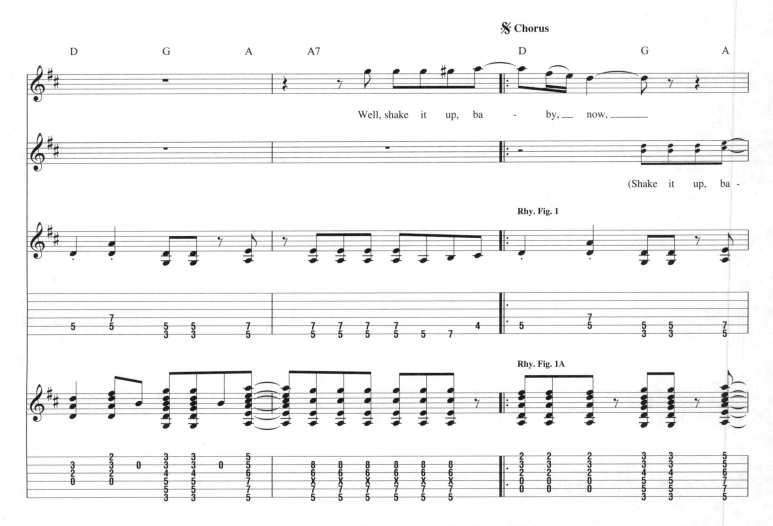

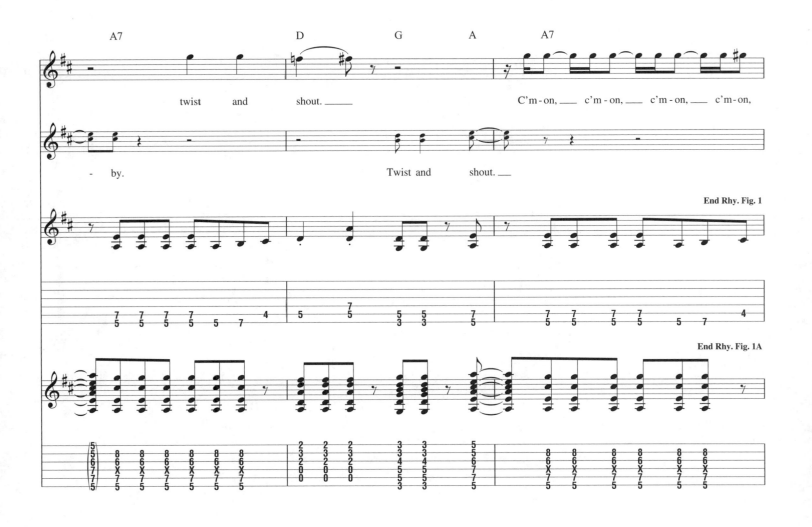

twist and shout. _____ C'm-on, _____ c'm-on, _____ c'm-on, _____ c'm-on,

- by. Twist and shout. ___

End Rhy. Fig. 1

End Rhy. Fig. 1A

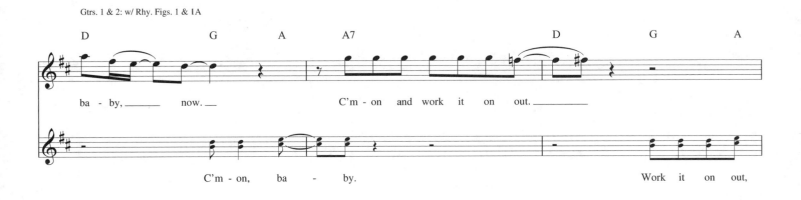

Gtrs. 1 & 2: w/ Rhy. Figs. 1 & 1A

ba - by, _____ now. __ C'm - on and work it on out. _____

C'm - on, ba - by. Work it on out,

Verse

1st time, Gtrs. 1 & 2: w/ Rhy. Figs. 1 & 1A (2 times)
2nd time, Gtrs. 1 & 2: w/ Rhy. Figs. 1 & 1A (1 3/4 times)
3rd time, Gtrs. 1 & 2: w/ Rhy. Figs. 1 & 1A (3 times)

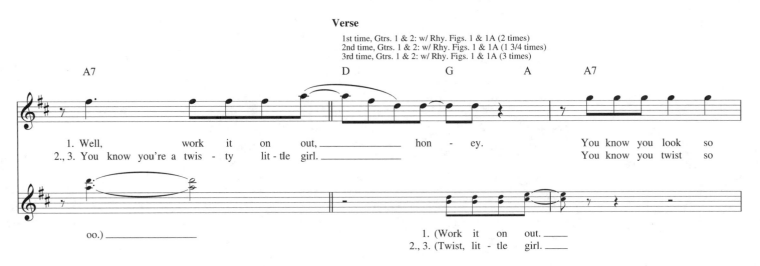

1. Well, work it on out, _____ hon - ey. You know you look so
2., 3. You know you're a twis - ty lit - tle girl. _____ You know you twist so

oo.) _____

1. (Work it on out. ___
2., 3. (Twist, lit - tle girl. ___

*Chord symbols reflect basic harmony, next 8 meas.

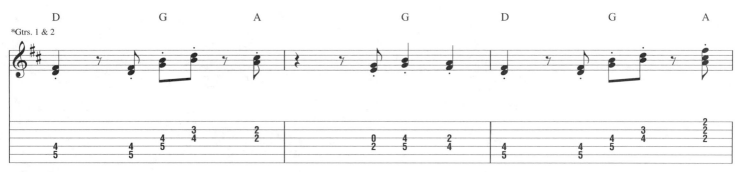

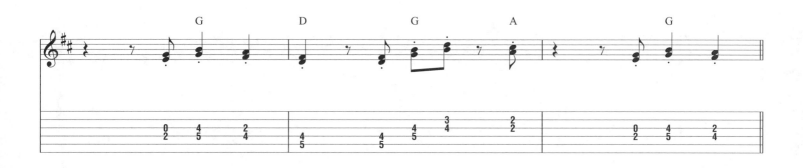

Bridge

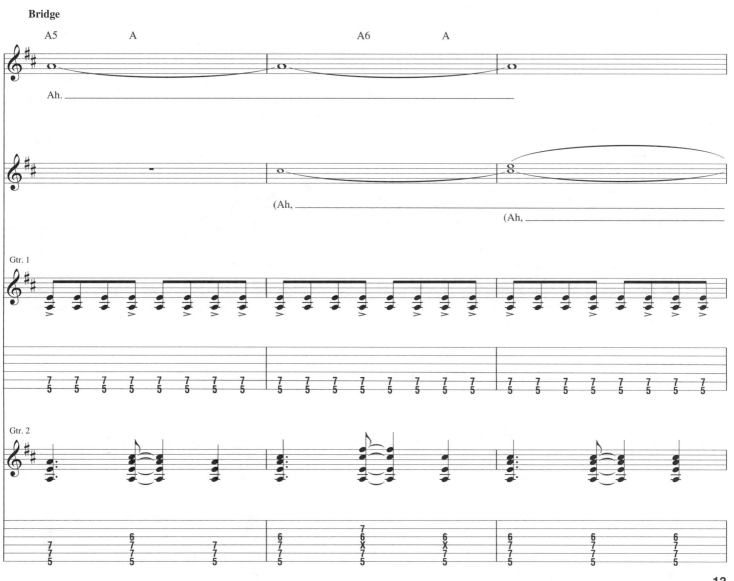

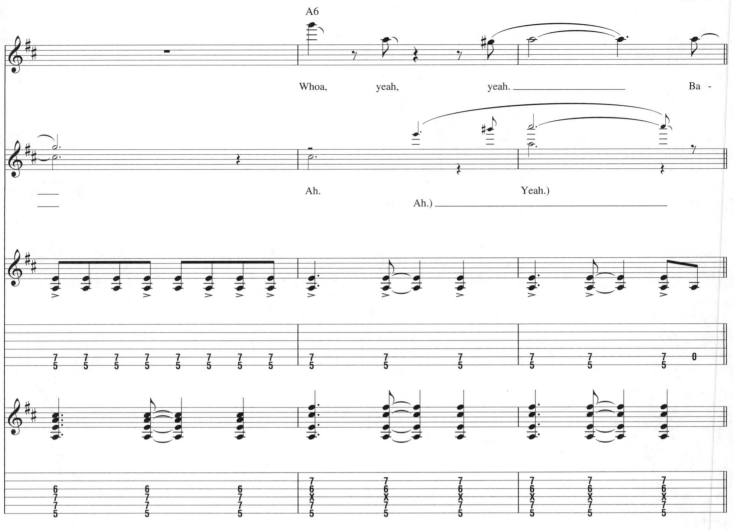

Whoa, yeah, yeah._____ Ba -

Ah.

Ah.)_____ Yeah.)

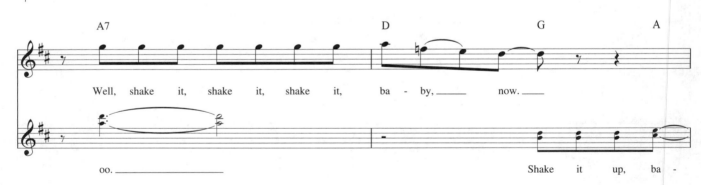

Coda

A7

Well, shake it, shake it, shake it, ba - by,____ now.____

oo._____

Shake it up, ba -

A7   D   G   A   A7

Well, shake it, shake it, shake it, ba - by,___ now.___   Well, shake it, shake it, shake it,

- by.   Shake it up, ba - by.

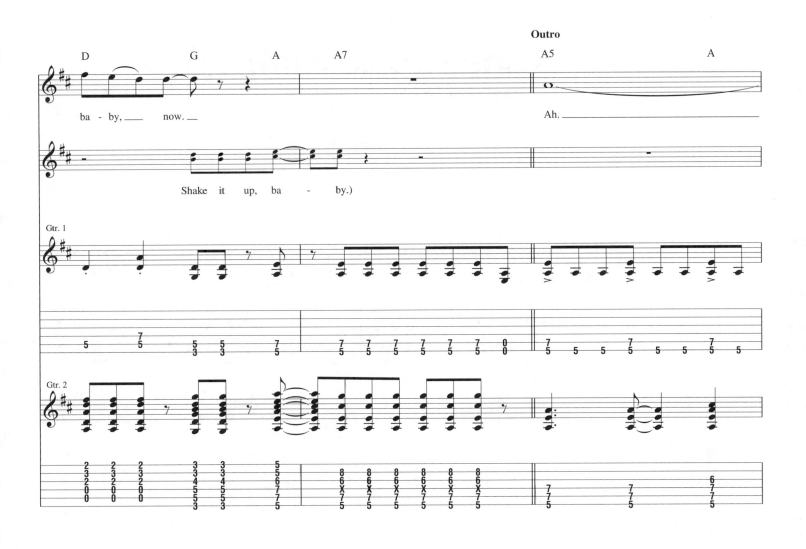

Anna (Go to Him)

Words and Music by Arthur Alexander

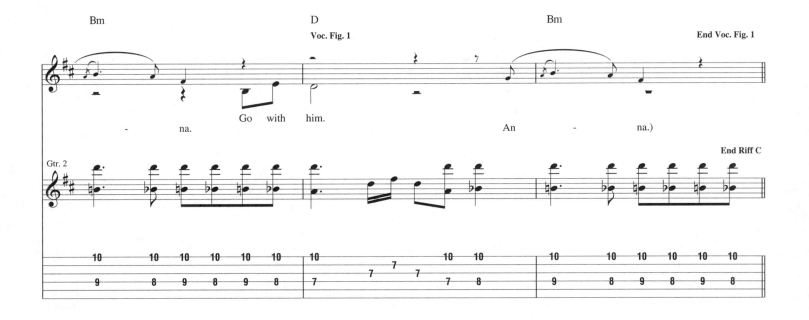

Voc. Fig. 1

End Voc. Fig. 1

Go with him.

- na.

An - na.)

End Riff C

Verse

Gtr. 1: w/ Rhy. Fig. 1 (3 times)
Gtr. 2: w/ Riff B (3 times)

2. An - na, ____ girl, ____ be - fore you go now, ____

I want you to know, now, ____ that I still

Rhy. Fig. 3

love you so. ____ But if he loves you more, ____ go with him.

w/ pick

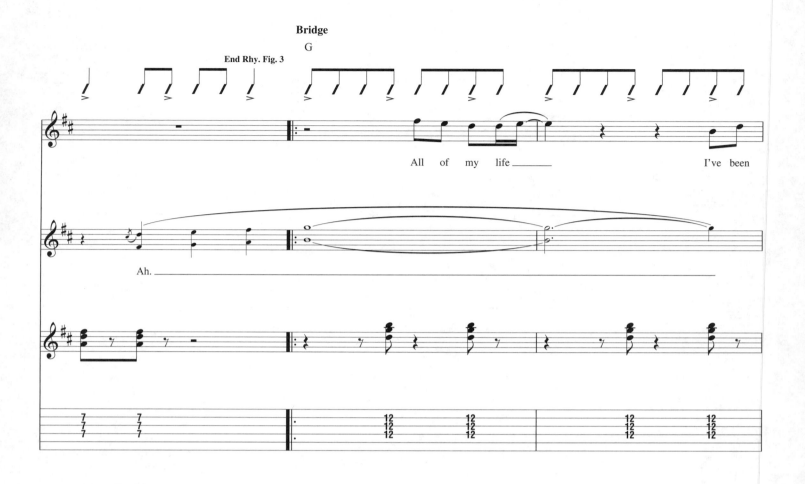

Bridge

All of my life _____ I've been

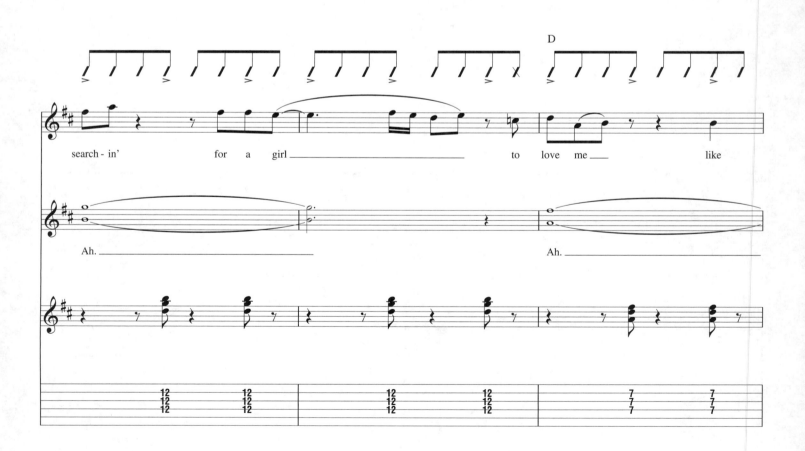

search-in' for a girl _____ to love me _____ like

leave me __ sad. What am I, what am I sup-posed __ to

Ah.

do? __ Oh, oh, oh, oh, oh, oh. 3., 4. An - na, __

Ah.

just one more thing girl, __ you give back your

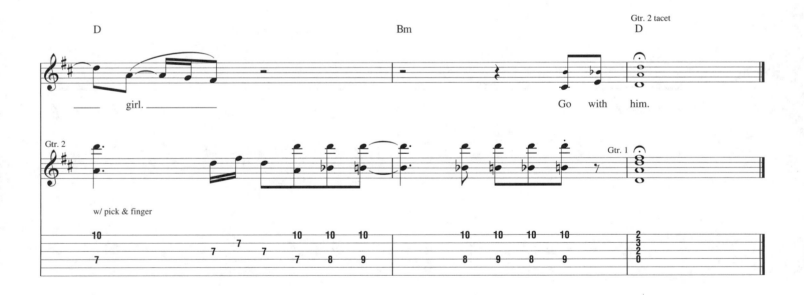

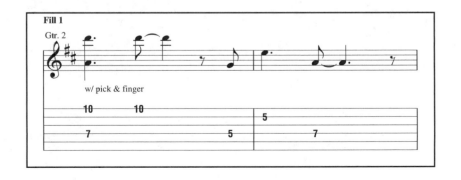

from *The Early Beatles*

Chains

Words and Music by Gerry Goffin and Carole King

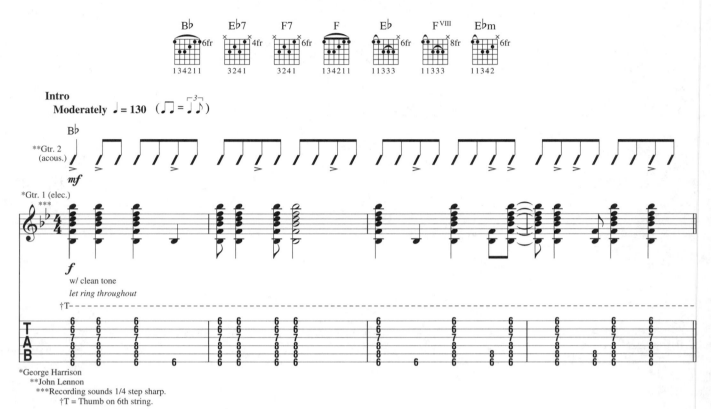

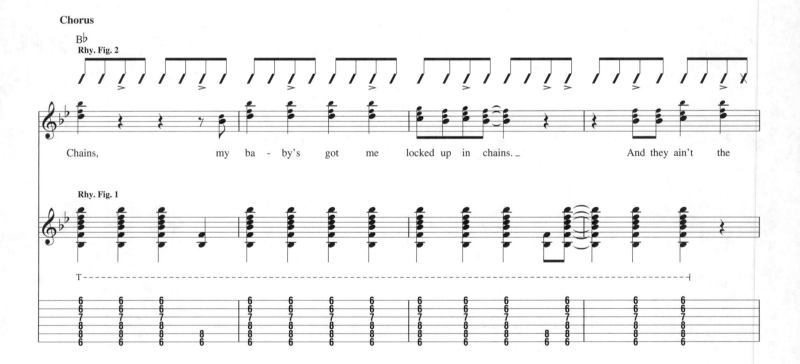

*George Harrison
**John Lennon
***Recording sounds 1/4 step sharp.
†T = Thumb on 6th string.

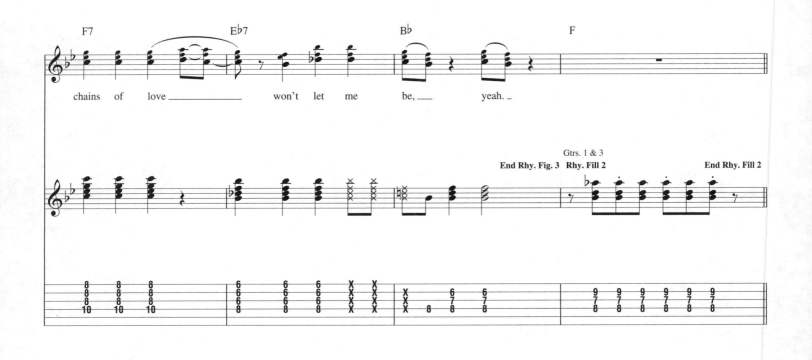

chains of love _____ won't let me be, __ yeah. _

Verse

1. I wan-na tell you, pret-ty _____ ba - by, _____ I _____ think you're fine. _____
2. Please be-lieve me when I _____ tell _____ you, _____ your _____ lips _____ are sweet. _____

Chorus

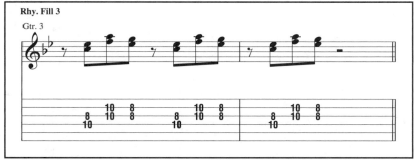

Outro-Chorus

from *The Early Beatles*

Boys

Words and Music by Luther Dixon and Wes Farrell

Guitar Solo

(cont. in slashes)

Outro-Chorus

Gtr. 2: w/ Riff B
Bkgd. Voc.: w/ Voc. Fig. 1 (till fade)

from *The Early Beatles*

Ask Me Why

Words and Music by John Lennon and Paul McCartney

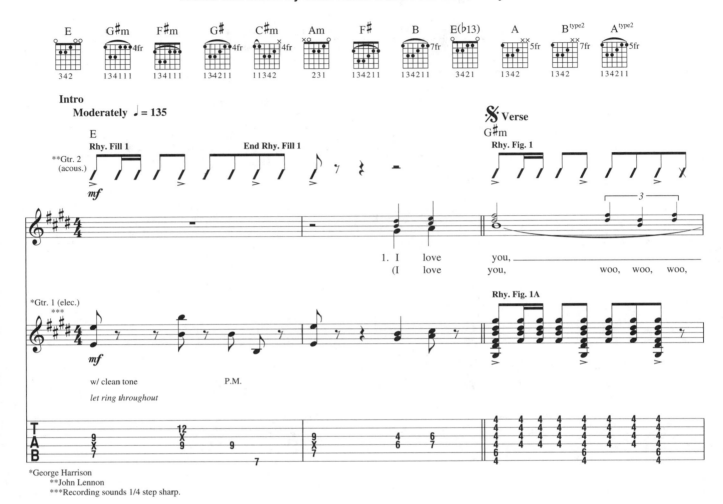

*George Harrison
**John Lennon
***Recording sounds 1/4 step sharp.

true, _____ that it real-ly on-ly goes to show, _
true, _____ woo, woo, woo, woo.)

End Rhy. Fig. 1A

that I know, _ that I, I, I, I _____ should
(Oo. _____

Rhy. Fill 2

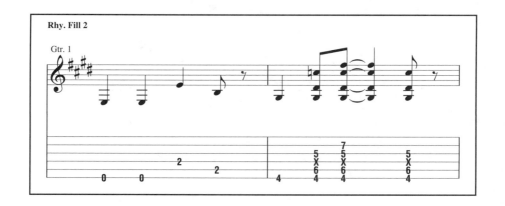

Please Please Me

Words and Music by John Lennon and Paul McCartney

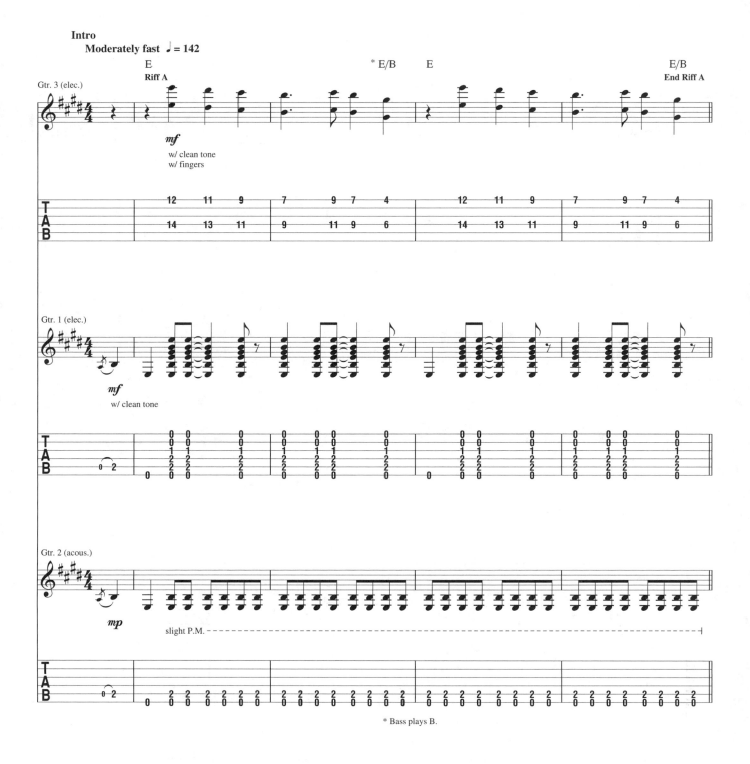

* Bass plays B.

% Verse

3rd time, Gtr. 3: w/ Fill 2   Gtr. 3 tacet   2nd time, Gtr. 1: w/ Rhy. Fill 1

E   A   E   G   A   B

1., 3. Last night I said these words to my _____ girl,
2. You don't need me to show the way, _____ love.

Fill 1   **End Fill 1**

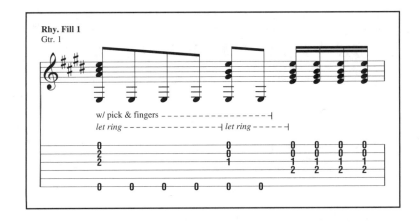

Rhy. Fill 1
Gtr. 1

w/ pick & fingers ----------------
let ring -------------- *let ring* ------

Fill 2
Gtr. 3

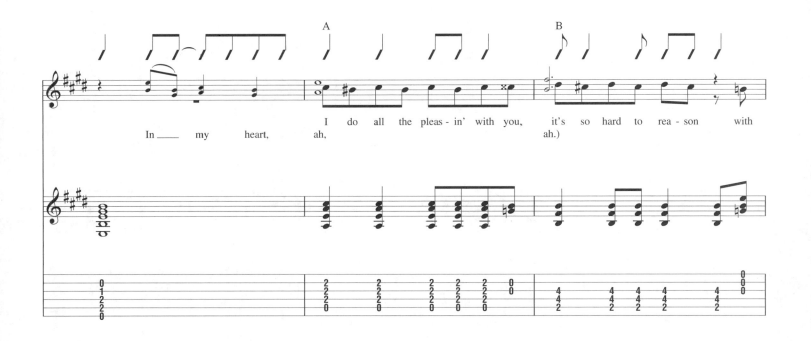

In ___ my heart, ah,   I do all the pleas - in' with you,   it's so hard to rea - son with ah.)

you,   oh, ___ yeah.   Why do you make me blue?

D.S. al Coda

(cont. in notation)

Gtr. 3

Gtr. 1

from *The Early Beatles*

P.S. I Love You
Words and Music by John Lennon and Paul McCartney

*John Lennon
**Recording sounds 1/4 step sharp.

††Gtr. 2 (clean) George Harrison - played *mf* .
Composite arrangement

48

Baby, It's You

Words and Music by Mack David, Burt Bacharach and Barney Williams

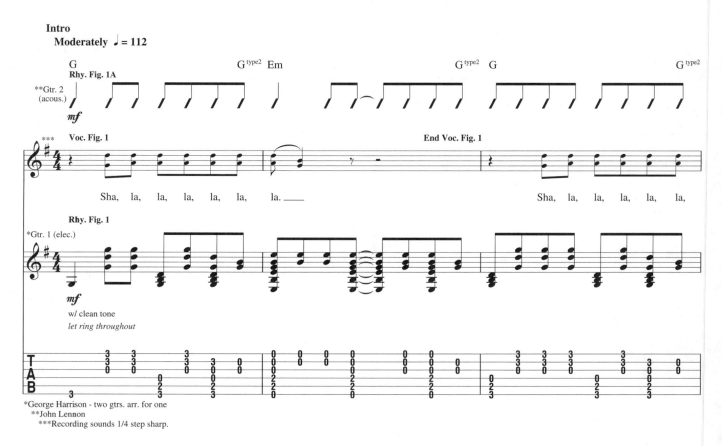

*George Harrison - two gtrs. arr. for one
**John Lennon
***Recording sounds 1/4 step sharp.

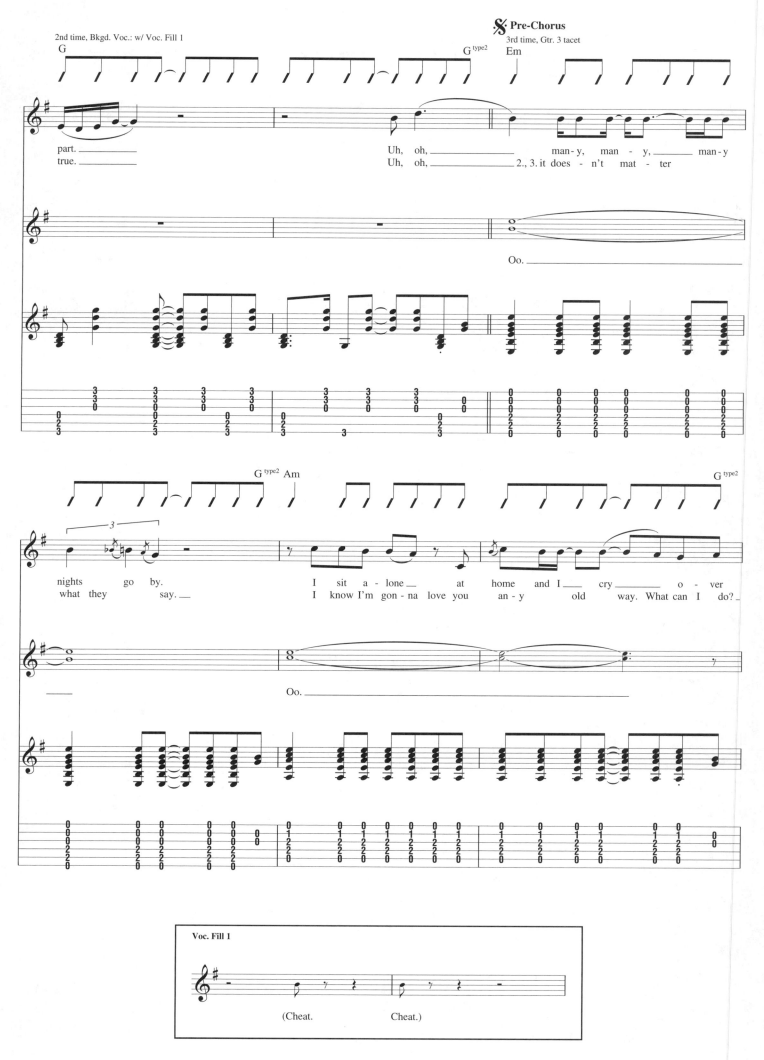

54

from *The Early Beatles*
A Taste of Honey

Words by Ric Marlow
Music by Bobby Scott

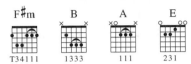

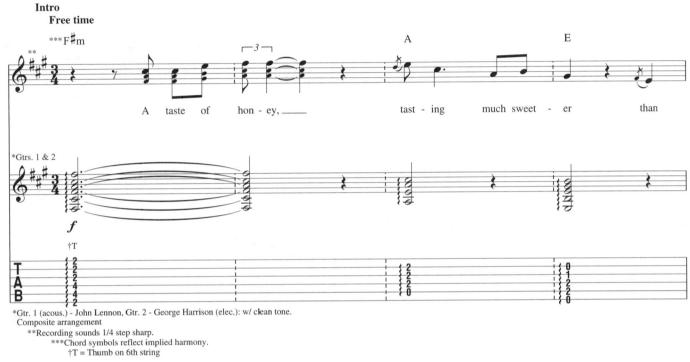

*Gtr. 1 (acous.) - John Lennon, Gtr. 2 - George Harrison (elec.): w/ clean tone.
Composite arrangement
**Recording sounds 1/4 step sharp.
***Chord symbols reflect implied harmony.
†T = Thumb on 6th string

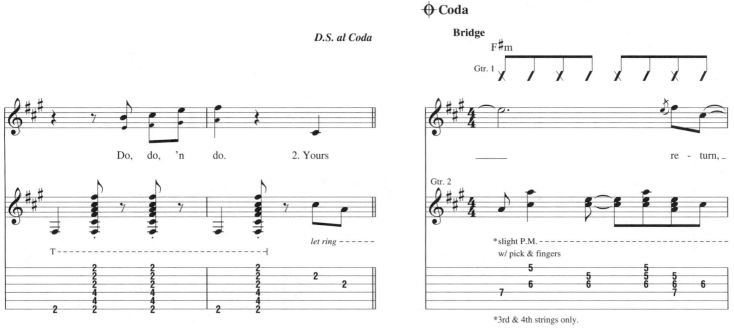

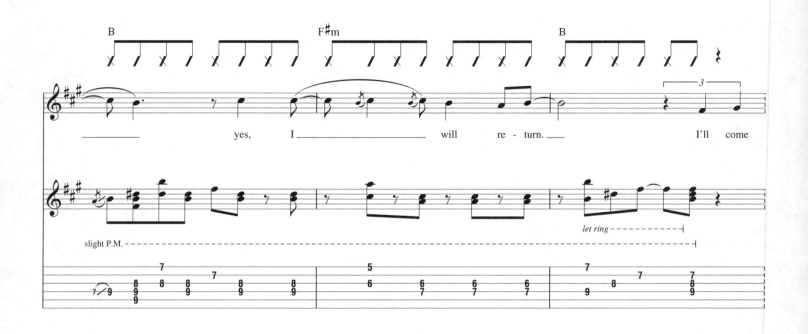

yes, I _____ will re - turn. _____ I'll come

slight P.M. -

let ring - - - - - - - - - -

Free time

Gtr. 1 tacet

back for the _____ hon - ey and

(He'll come back for the _____ hon - ey.)

Gtr. 2

w/ pick

let ring -

Outro
Faster ♩ = 112

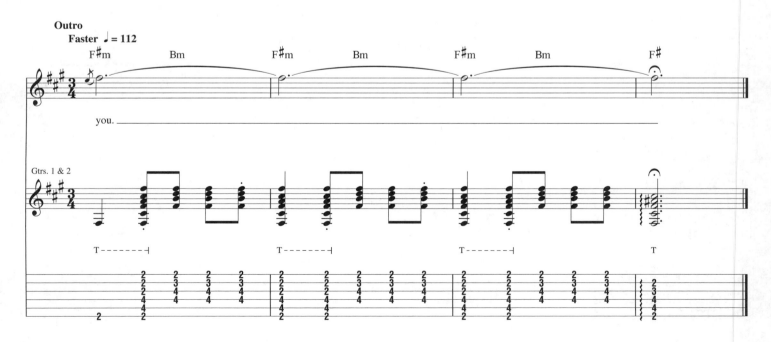

you. _____

Gtrs. 1 & 2

Do You Want to Know a Secret?

Words and Music by John Lennon and Paul McCartney

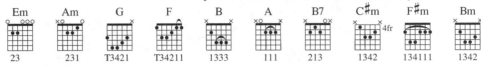

Em   Am   G   F   B   A   B7   C#m   F#m   Bm

Tune down 1/4 step

Intro
Free time

You'll nev-er know how much I real-ly love you.   You'll nev-er know how much I

w/ clean tone
let ring throughout

*George Harrison

**Gtr. 1 (elec.) w/ clean tone - George Harrison
Gtr. 2 (acous.) - John Lennon
Composite arrangement

Verse

Gtr. 3 tacet
2nd & 3rd times, Bkgd. Voc.: w/ Voc. Fig. 1 (3 times)
2nd & 3rd times, Gtrs. 1 & 2: w/ Rhy. Fill 1

E   Abm7   Gm7

Moderately ♩ = 124

F   B

real-ly care.   1., 3., 5. Lis-ten,

(cont. in notation)

Gtr. 3
Gtrs. 1 & 2
divisi
Gtrs. 1 & 2

Voc. Fig. 1

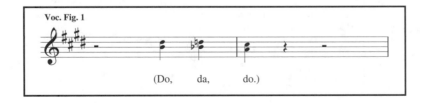

(Do, da, do.)

from *Beatles VI*

Kansas City/Hey Hey Hey Hey

Intro
Moderately fast ♩ = 130

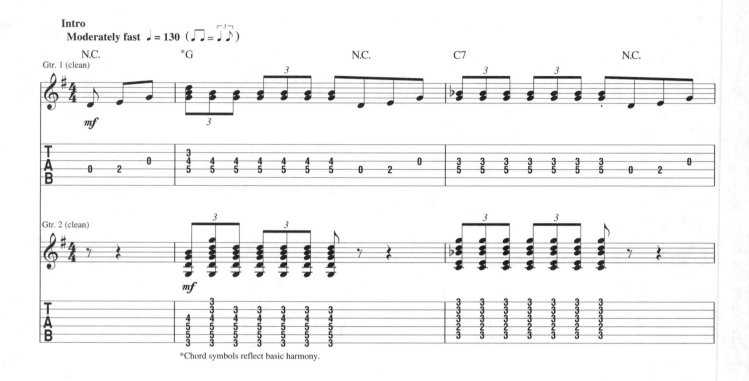

*Chord symbols reflect basic harmony.

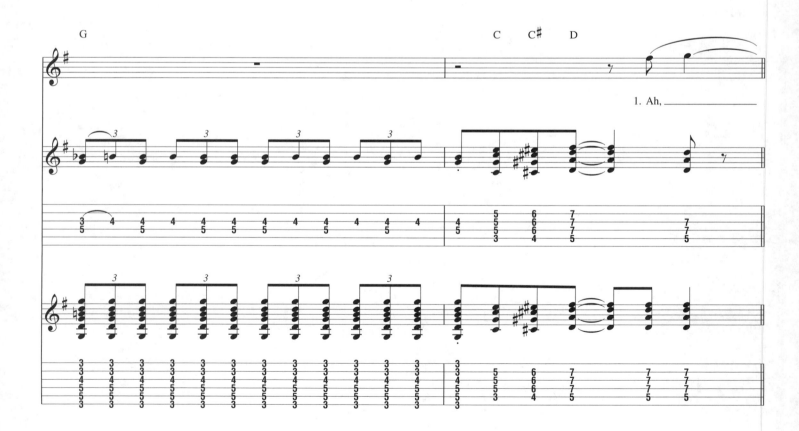

KANSAS CITY
Words and Music by Jerry Leiber and Mike Stoller

Guitar Solo

Gtr. 2: w/ Rhy. Fig. 1

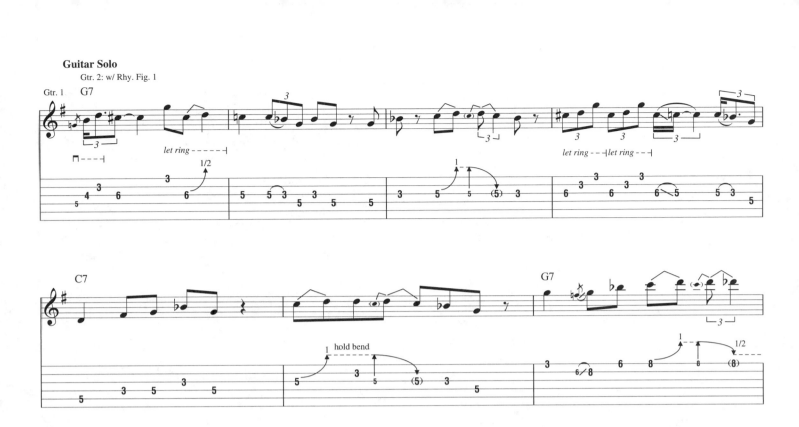

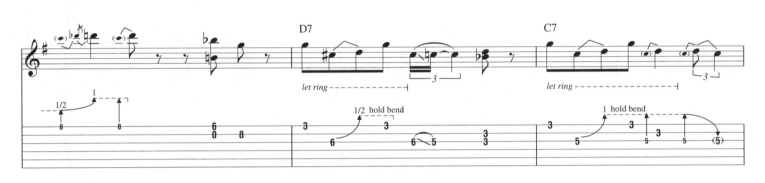

3. Hey,   hey,   hey,

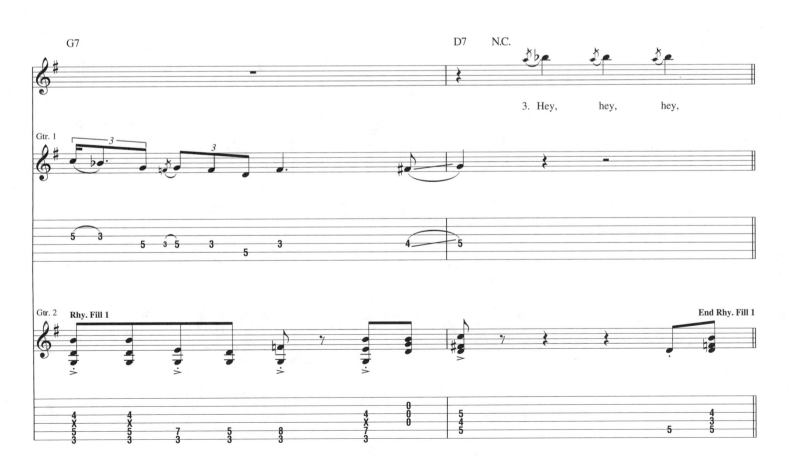

HEY HEY HEY HEY
Words and Music by Richard Penniman

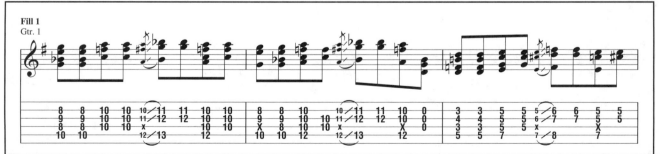

Outro

Eight Days a Week

Words and Music by John Lennon and Paul McCartney

*Chord symbols reflect basic harmony.

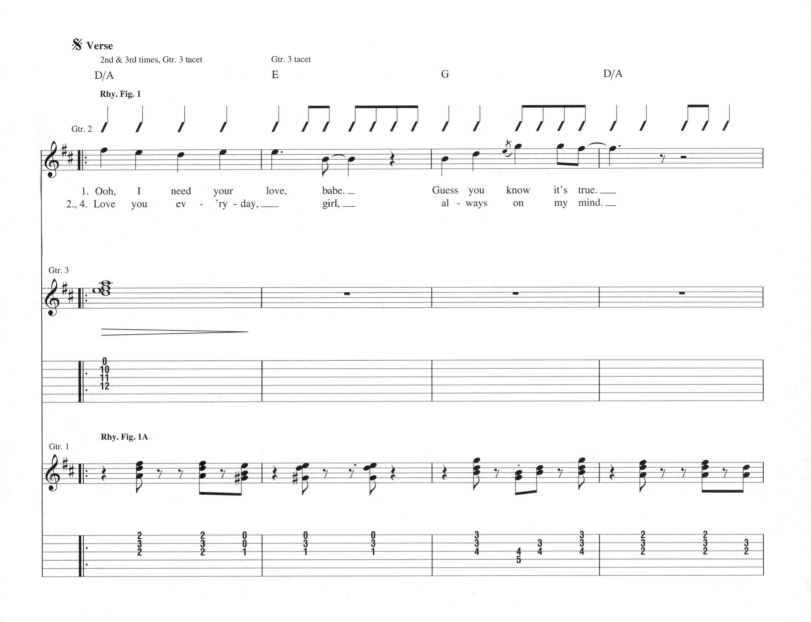

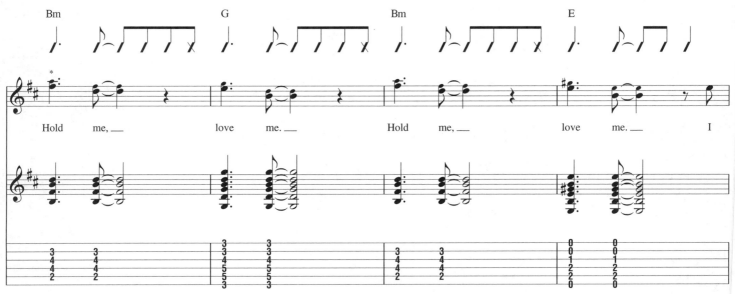

Bm   G   Bm   E

Hold me, ___ love me. ___ Hold me, ___ love me. ___ I

*Harm. voc. sung 2nd & 3rd times only (next 4 meas.).

To Coda ⊕

D/A   E   G   D/A

End Rhy. Fig. 1

ain't got noth-in' but love, { 1., 4. babe, ___ } eight days a week. ___
                              { 2. girl, ___ }

End Rhy. Fig. 1A

Bridge

A   Bm

Rhy. Fig. 2

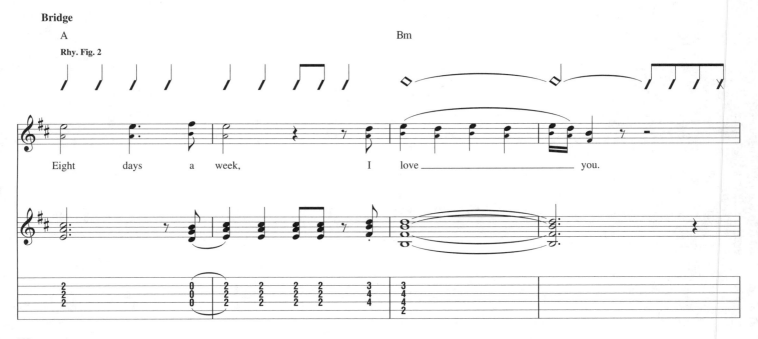

Eight days a week, I love _____ you.

Eight days a week is not e-nough to show I care.

Coda

Outro

Eight days a week.

let ring -

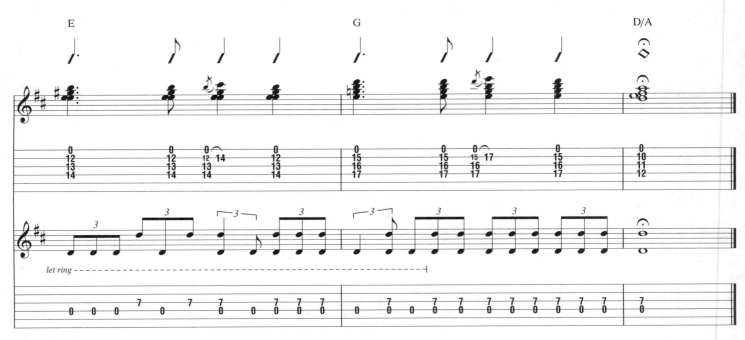

let ring - - - - - - - - - - - - - - - -

You Like Me Too Much

Words and Music by George Harrison

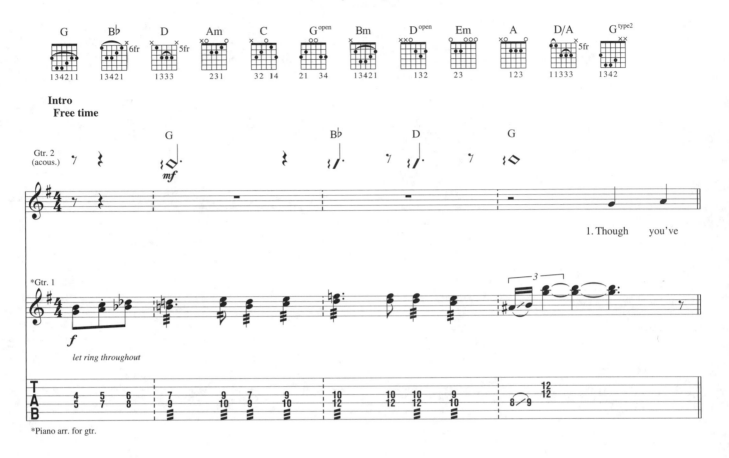

*Piano arr. for gtr.

**Hohner Pianet arr. for gtr.

76

78

'Cause you

steady gliss.

could-n't real - ly stand ___ it, I'd ad - mit ___ that I was wrong. ___ I

Chorus

Gtr. 2: w/ Rhy. Fig. 2

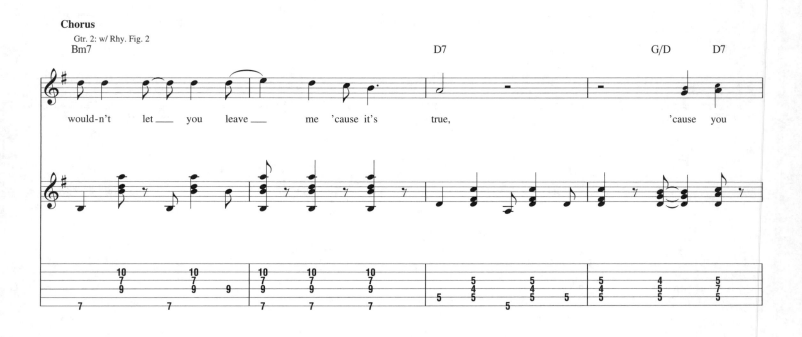

would-n't let ___ you leave ___ me 'cause it's true, 'cause you

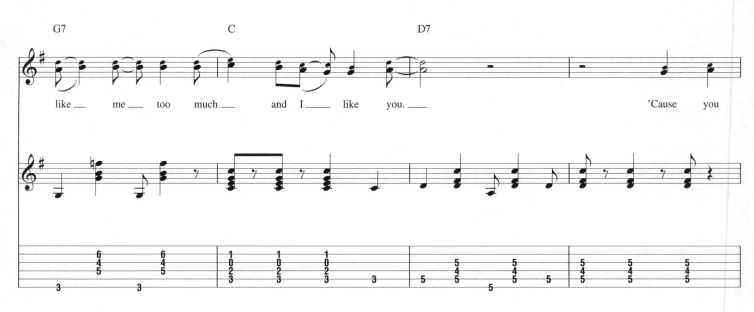

like ___ me ___ too much ___ and I ___ like you. ___ 'Cause you

like — me too much — and I — like you. —

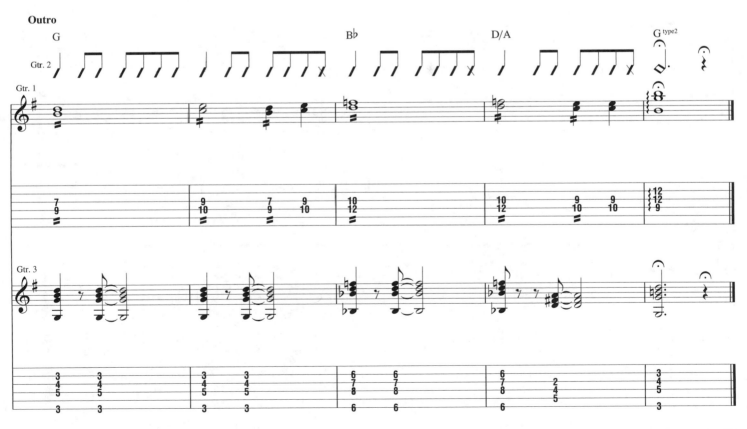

Outro

Bad Boy

By Larry Williams

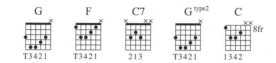

Intro
Moderately fast ♩ = 136

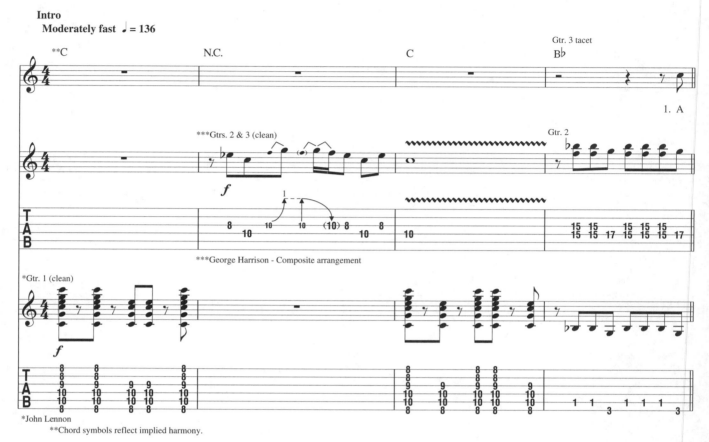

*George Harrison - Composite arrangement

*Gtr. 1 (clean)

*John Lennon
**Chord symbols reflect implied harmony.

Verse

bad lit-tle kid moved in-to my neigh-bor-hood. ___ He

Ld. Voc.: w/ ad lib. screams (next 7 meas.)

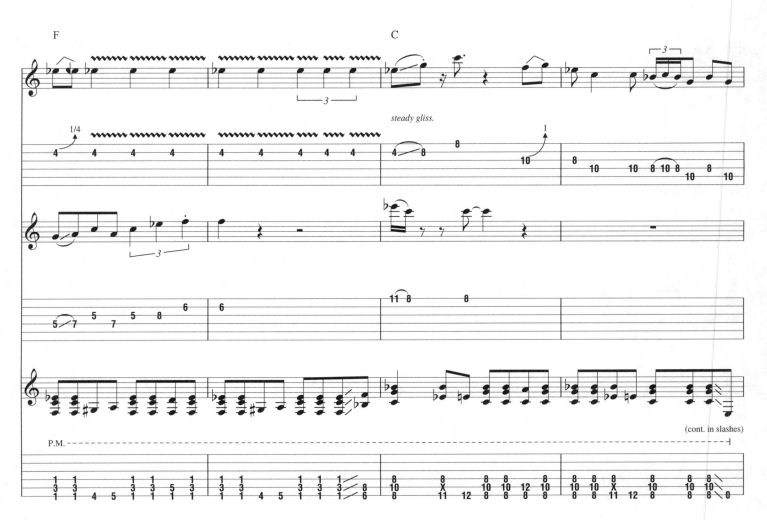

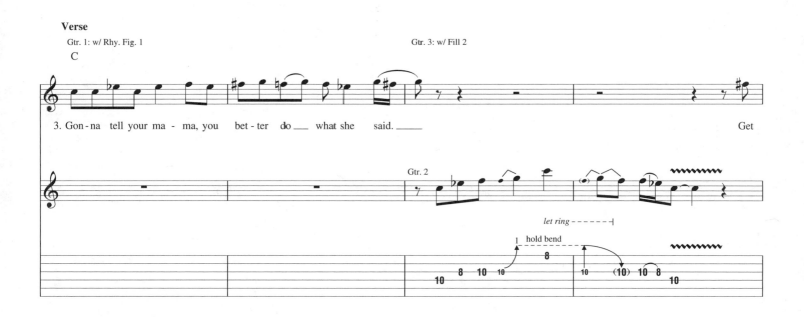

Verse

from *Beatles VI*

I Don't Want to Spoil the Party

Words and Music by John Lennon and Paul McCartney

G   D/A   Em   B7   Am   F   A   C

Gtr. 1: Drop D tuning:
(low to high) D-A-D-G-B-E

*George Harrison

**John Lennon
***Chord symbols reflect implied harmony.

(cont. in slashes)

Verse

wan-na spoil the par-ty, so I'll go. I would hate

†P.M. 6th & 5th strings throughout.

my dis-ap-point-ment to show. There's

noth-in' for me here, so I will dis-ap-pear. If she turns

Oo.

93

Verse

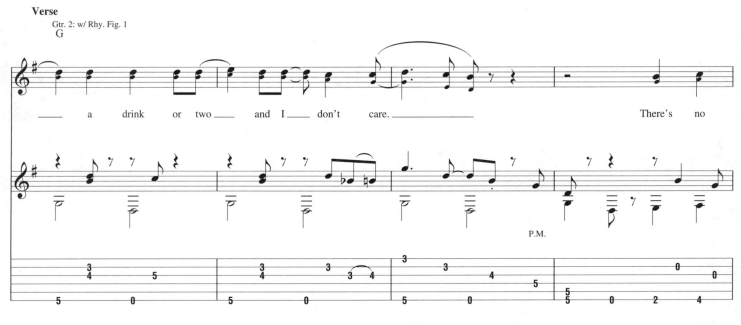

98

think I'll take a walk ___ and look for her. ___

Outro

from *Beatles VI*

Words of Love

Words and Music by Buddy Holly

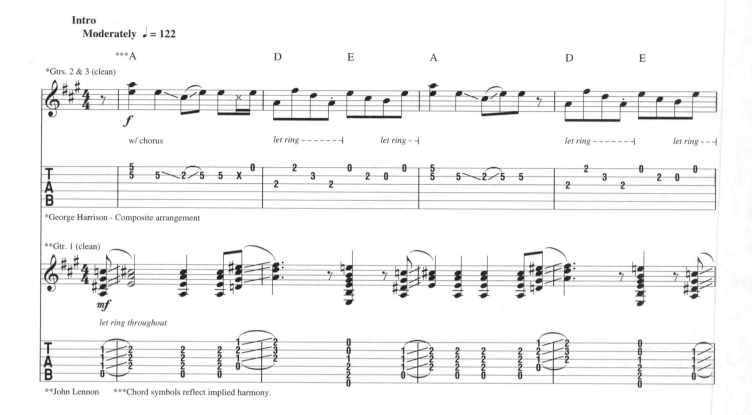

*George Harrison - Composite arrangement

**John Lennon   ***Chord symbols reflect implied harmony.

Verse

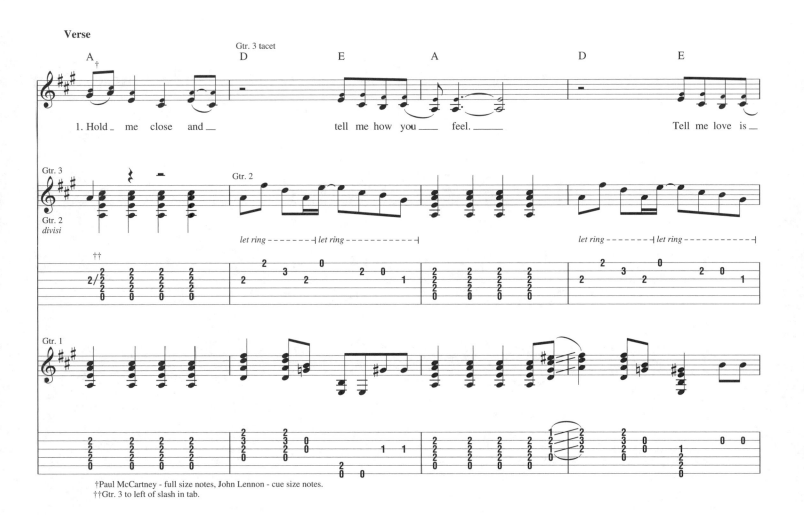

†Paul McCartney - full size notes, John Lennon - cue size notes.
††Gtr. 3 to left of slash in tab.

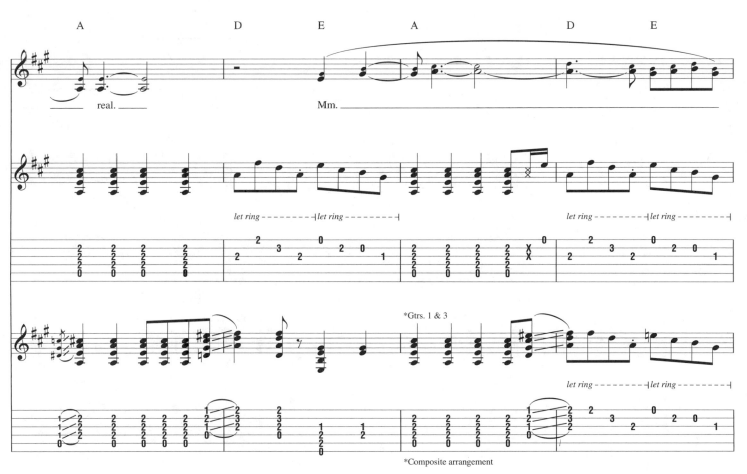

*Composite arrangement

Words __ of love you __ whis-per soft and __ true. Dar-ling, I love __

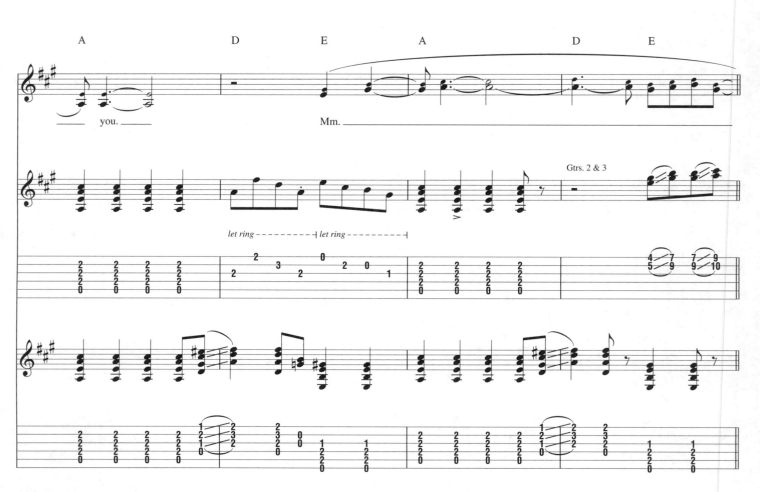

__ you. __ Mm. __ Dar-ling, I love __

Interlude

Verse

2. Let me hear you say the words I long to hear. Dar - ling, when you're near. Mm.

Gtr. 2

*Gtrs. 1 & 3

*Composite arrangement

Rhy. Fig. 1

End Rhy. Fig. 1

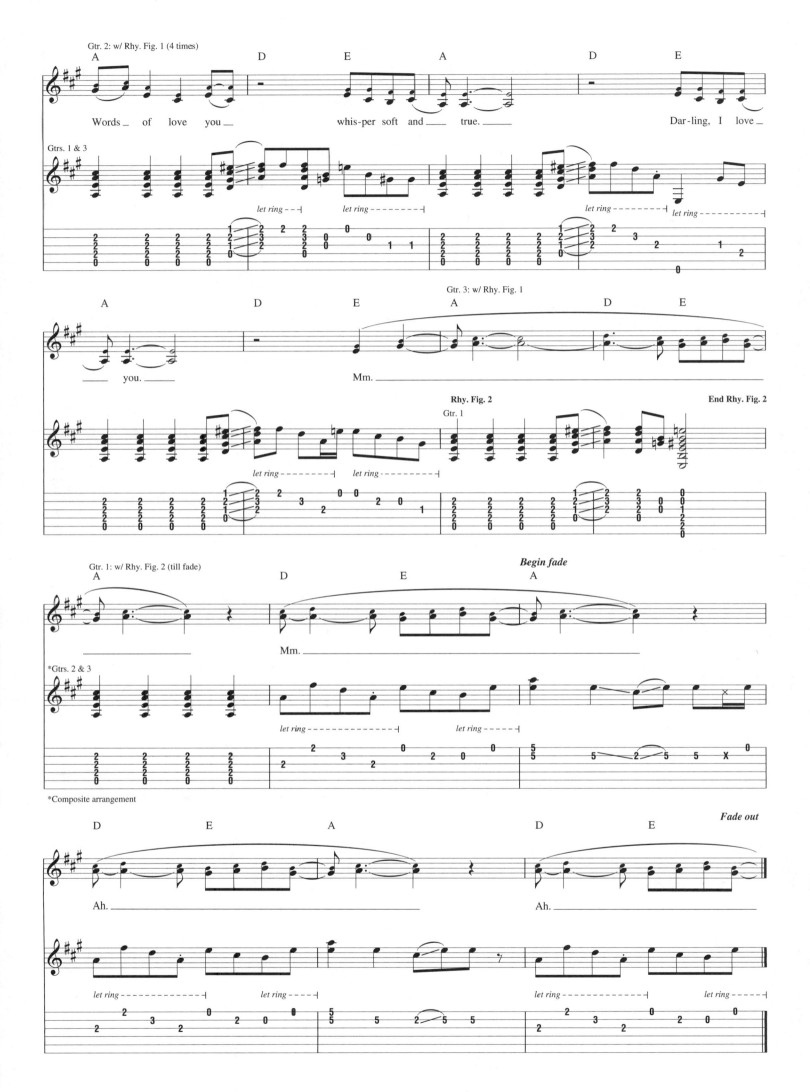

from *Beatles VI*

What You're Doing

Words and Music by John Lennon and Paul McCartney

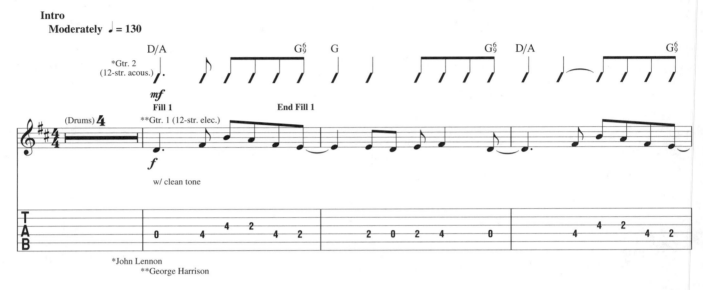

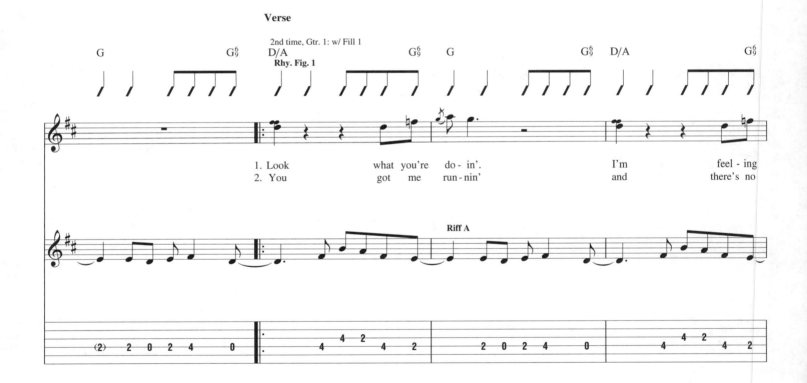

*John Lennon
**George Harrison

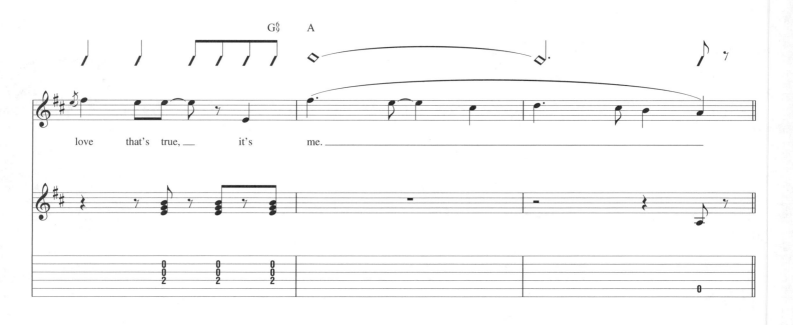

love that's true, ___ it's me. _____

Verse

Gtr. 1: w/ Fill 1
Gtr. 2: w/ Rhy. Fig. 1

Gtr. 1: w/ Riff A

D/A   G   D/A   G

3., 4. Please   stop your ly - in',   you've   got me cry - in', girl. ___ Why should it

To Coda

Chorus

1st time, Gtrs. 1 & 2: w/ Rhy. Figs. 2 & 2A
2nd time, Gtrs. 1 & 2: w/ Rhy. Figs. 2 & 2A (1st 2 meas.)
1st time, Bkgd. Vocs.: w/ Voc. Fig. 1
2nd time, Bkgd. Vocs.: w/ Voc. Fig. 1 (1st 2 meas.)

Bm   G   D/A   G

be so much ___ to ask of you, ___ what you're do - in' to ___ me? ___

Guitar Solo

Gtr. 2: w/ Rhy. Fig. 1

D/A   G   D/A   G

*George Harrison

do-in' to me? ___ What you're do-in' to ___ me. ___ What you're
Oo. ___

do - in'   to ___ me.
Oo.) _____

from *Beatles VI*

Yes It Is

Words and Music by John Lennon and Paul McCartney

Chorus

red   is the col-or ____   that my ba-by wore, ____   and what's more, ____   it's   true. ____   Yes, it   is.

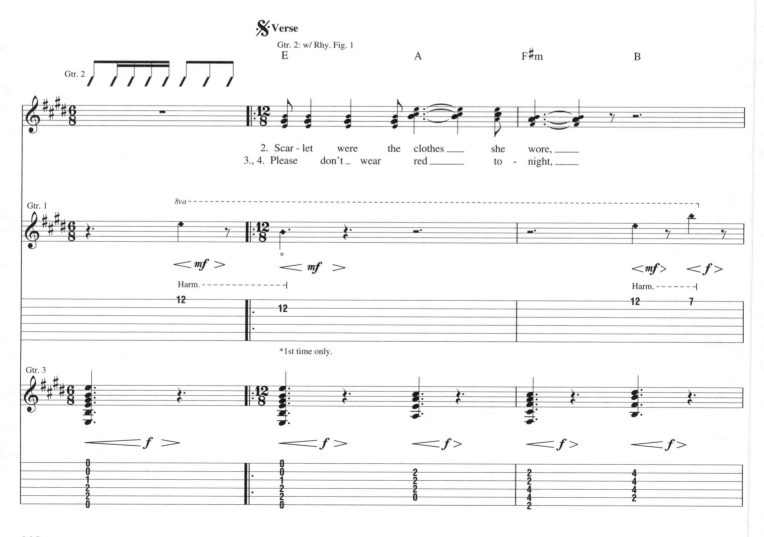

2. Scar-let   were   the   clothes ____   she   wore, ____
3., 4. Please   don't _ wear   red ____   to - night, ____

*1st time only.

Dizzy Miss Lizzie

Words and Music by Larry Williams

*Composite arrangement

**Chord symbols reflect basic harmony.

Woo!

Verse

3. You make me diz - zy, Miss Liz - zie,   when you   call   my __ name. _____
4. Run and tell   your ma - ma,   I   want you to   be   my   bride. _____

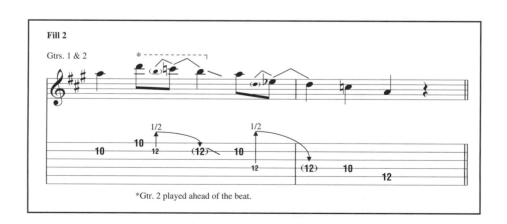

*Gtr. 2 played ahead of the beat.

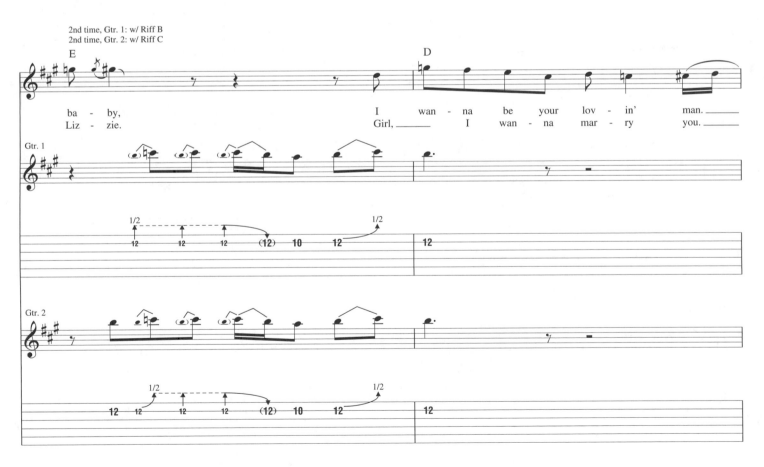

from *Beatles VI*

Tell Me What You See

Words and Music by John Lennon and Paul McCartney

tell me what you see. It is no sur - prise now,

Verse

2nd & 3rd times, Gtr. 2 tacet
3rd time, Gtr. 1: w/ Rhy. Fill 4

what you see is me.

2. Big and black the clouds may be,
3., 4. Lis - ten to me one more time,

2nd time, Gtr. 1: w/ Rhy. Fill 1
3rd time, Gtr. 1: w/ Rhy. Fill 5

time will pass a - way.
how can I get through?

If you put your trust in me
Can't you try to see that I'm

Rhy. Fill 1
Gtr. 1

Rhy. Fill 4
Gtr. 1

Rhy. Fill 5
Gtr. 1

122

from *Beatles VI*

Every Little Thing

Words and Music by John Lennon and Paul McCartney

And you know the __ things __ she does, she does for me, __ oo. __

Outro

Ev-'ry lit-tle thing, ___ ev-'ry lit-tle

Begin fade

thing, ___ ev-'ry lit-tle thing. ___

Fade out

Help!

Words and Music by John Lennon and Paul McCartney

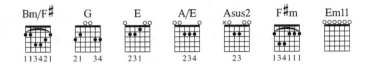

***Chord symbols reflect overall harmony.   †Sitar arr. for gtr.

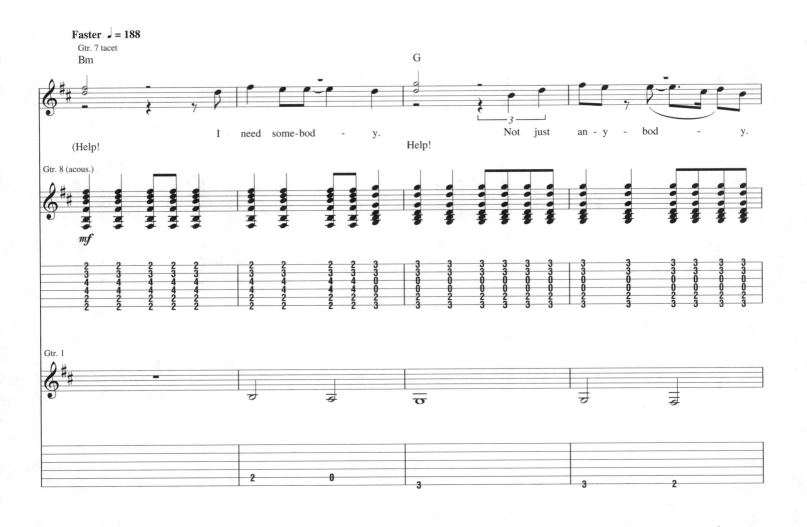

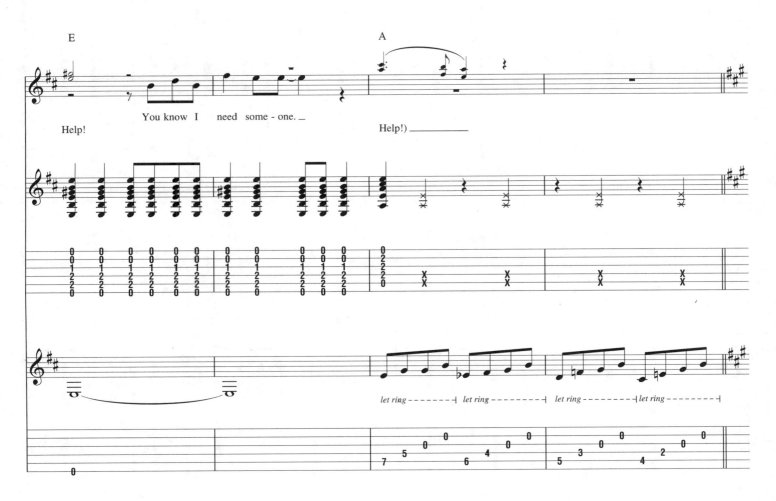

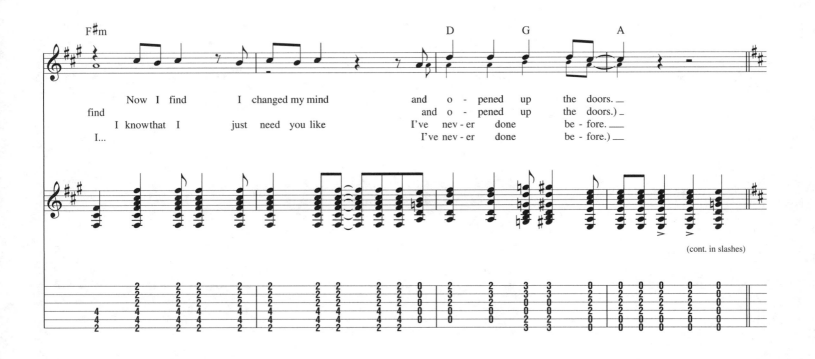

Now I find   I changed my mind   and o - pened up   the doors. __
find   and o - pened up   the doors.) __
I know that I   just need you like   I've nev - er   done   be - fore. __
I...   I've nev - er   done   be - fore.) __

(cont. in slashes)

𝄋 **Chorus**

Bm/F♯   G

Gtr. 8

Help   me if __ you   can, __   I'm   feel - in'   down. _____   And   I   do __

Gtr. 9 (elec.)

mf
w/ clean tone

Gtr. 1

ap - pre - ci - ate ___ you be - in' 'round. _____

Help me get ___ my feet ___ back on the ground. _____ Won't you

Gtr. 1: w/ Rhy. Fig. 1
Gtr. 8: w/ Rhy. Fig. 2

A

C#m

But now these days are gone ___ and I'm not so self as-

(Now _____ these days are gone. ___

F#m

sured. _____ Now I find I changed my mind and

And now I find and

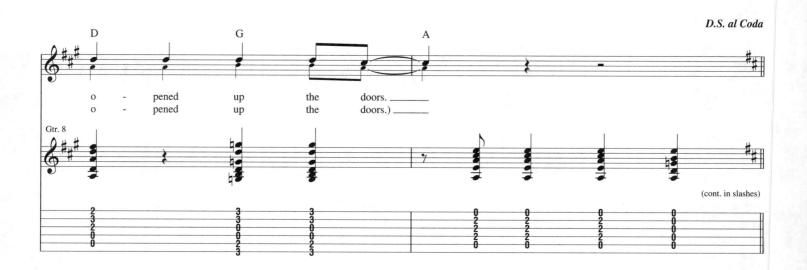

D   G   A

D.S. al Coda

o - pened up the doors. _____

o - pened up the doors.) _____

Gtr. 8

(cont. in slashes)

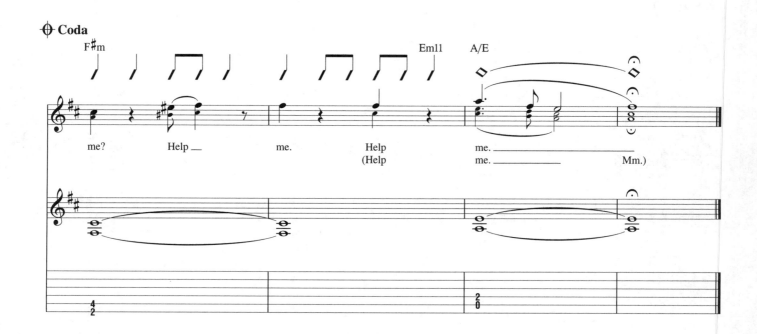

Coda

F#m   Em11   A/E

me?   Help ___ me.   Help   me. _____

(Help   me. _____ Mm.)

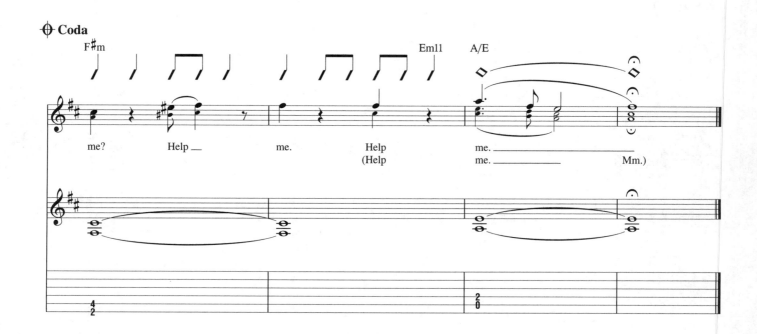

136

The Night Before

Words and Music by John Lennon and Paul McCartney

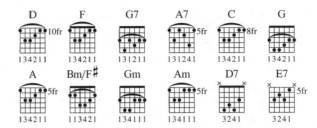

*Elec. piano (Hohner Pianet) arr. for gtr.

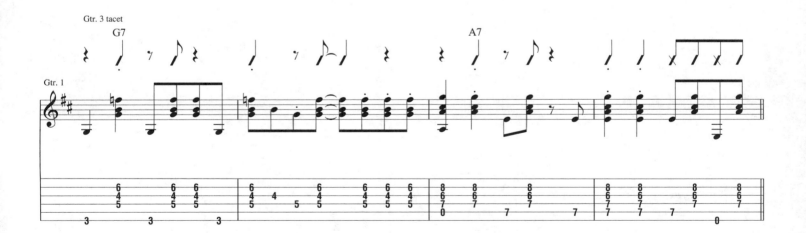

Verse

1. We said our good-byes. _____ (Ah, the night be-fore. _____
2. Were you tell-ing lies? _____

Love was in _____ your eyes. _____
Was I so un-wise? _____
_____ Ah, the night be-fore. _____

𝄋 Chorus

2nd time, Gtrs. 3 & 4 tacet

Now to-day _____ I find _____ you have changed _____ your mind.
When I held you near _____ you were so _____ sin -

138

Verse
1st time, Gtr. 1: w/ Rhy. Fig. 1
Gtr. 2: w/ Rhy. Fig. 1A
2nd time, Gtr. 1: w/ Rhy. Fill 2

2nd time, Gtr. 1: w/ Rhy. Fig. 1 (last 6 meas.)

Chorus
1st time, Gtrs. 1 & 2: w/ Rhy. Figs. 2 & 2A
2nd time, Gtrs. 1 & 2: w/ Rhy. Figs. 2 & 2A (1st 6 meas.)

Rhy. Fill 2
Gtr. 1

Guitar Solo

Gtr. 2: w/ Rhy. Fig. 1A (1st 4 meas., 2 times)

Coda

oh, like the night be - fore.

let ring -

from *Help! Original Motion Picture Soundtrack*

You've Got To Hide Your Love Away

Words and Music by John Lennon and Paul McCartney

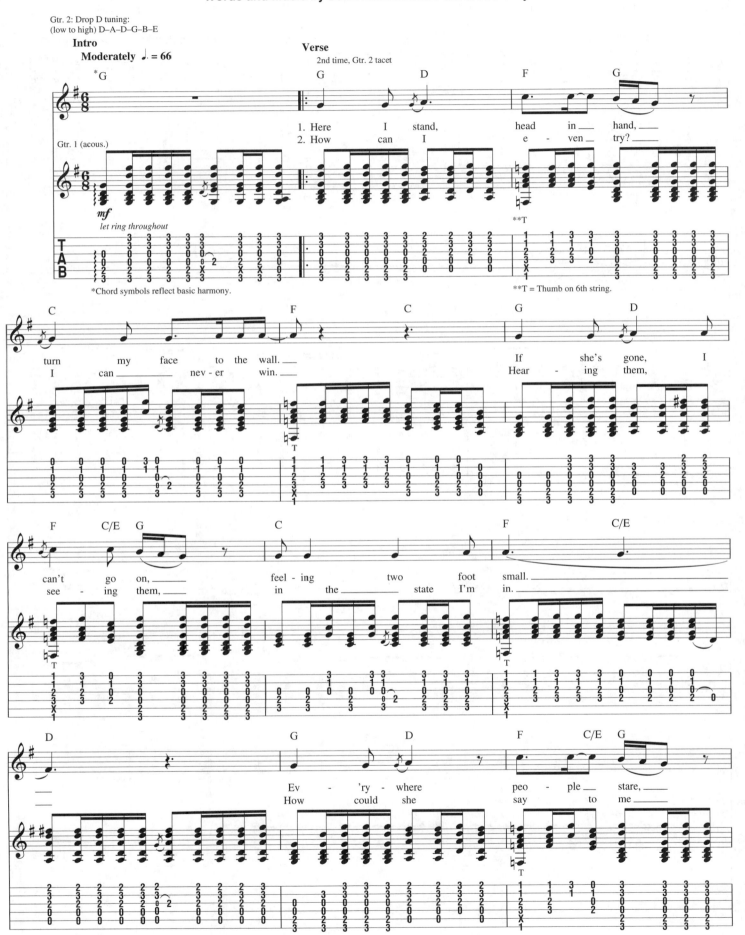

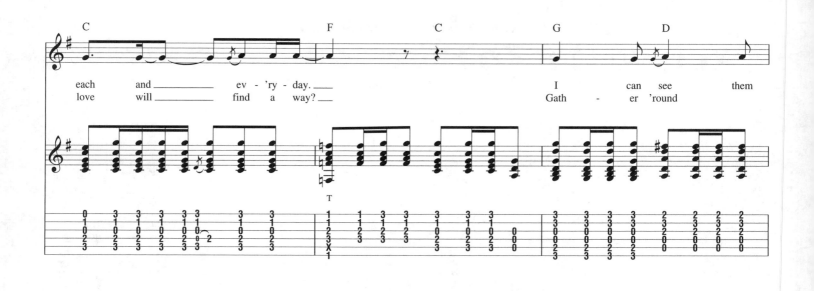

each and _____ ev - 'ry - day. _____   I   can   see   them
love will _____ find   a   way? _____   Gath - er 'round

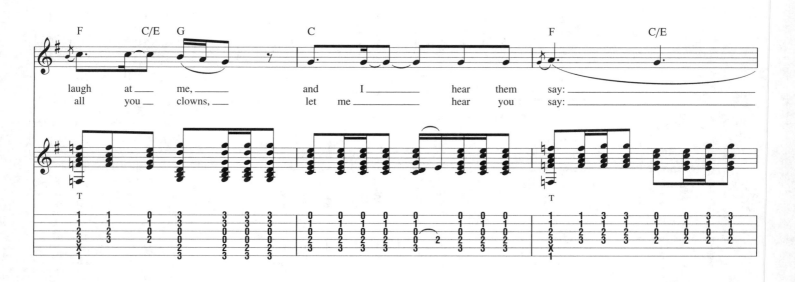

laugh   at ____ me, ____   and   I _____ hear   them   say: _____
all   you ____ clowns, ____   let   me _____ hear   you   say: _____

Chorus

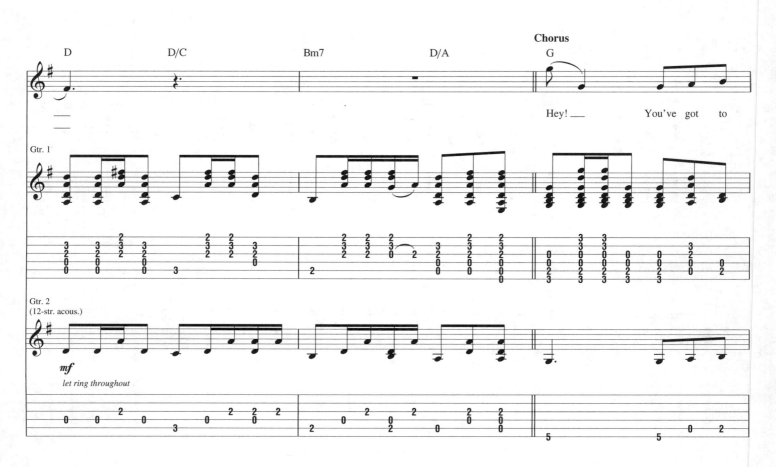

____   Hey! ____   You've   got   to

Gtr. 1

Gtr. 2
(12-str. acous.)

mf
let ring throughout

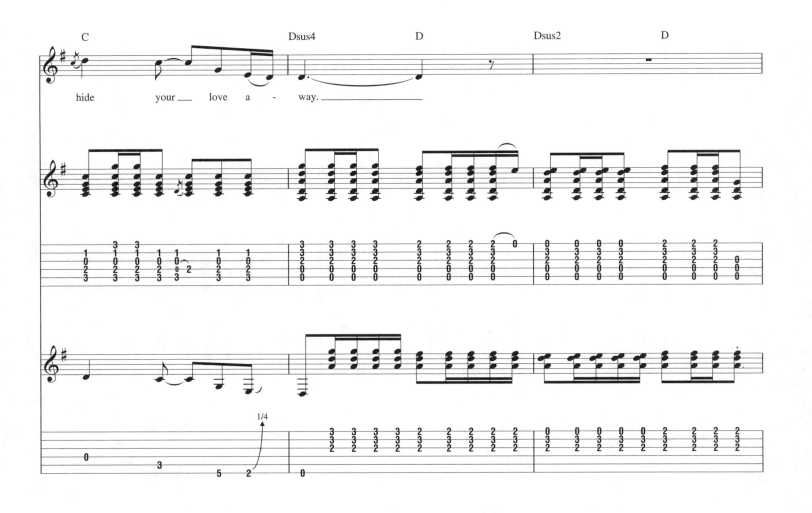

hide   your __ love a - way. _____

Hey! __   You've got to hide   your __ love a - way.

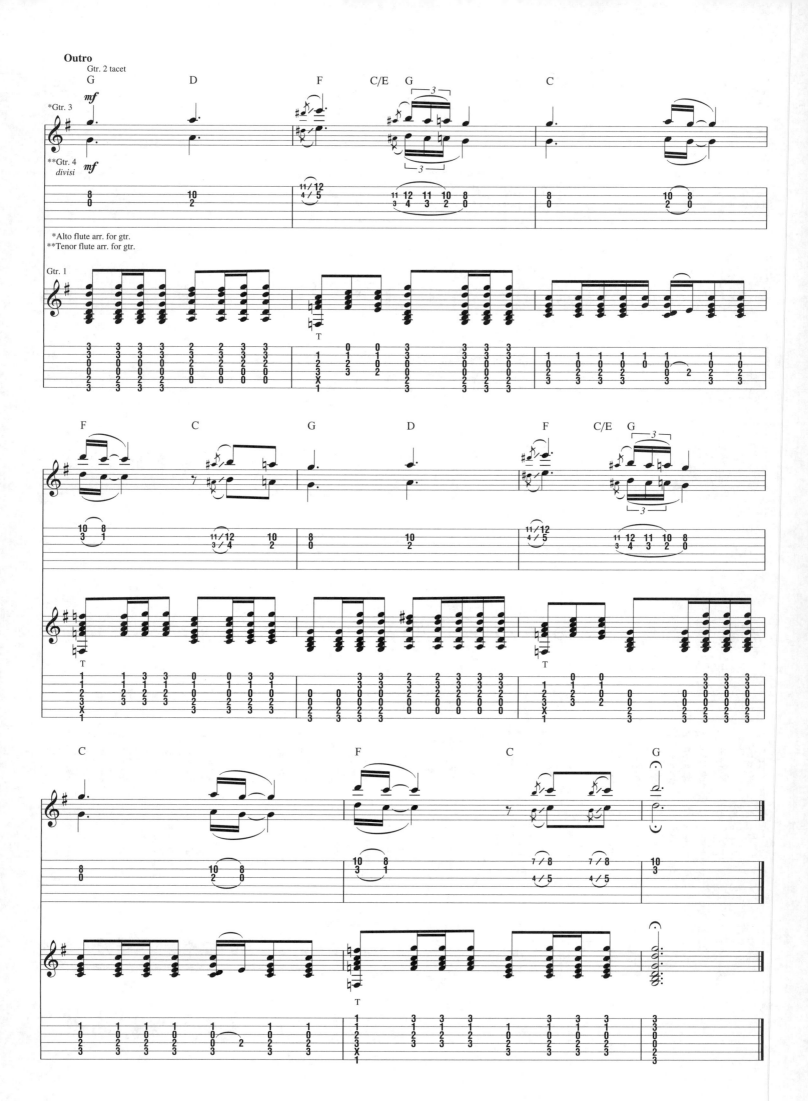

I Need You

Words and Music by George Harrison

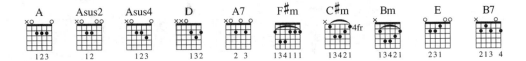

*Recording sounds 1/4 step flat.

**Vol. swells (George Harrison plays chords while John Lennon turns vol. knob).

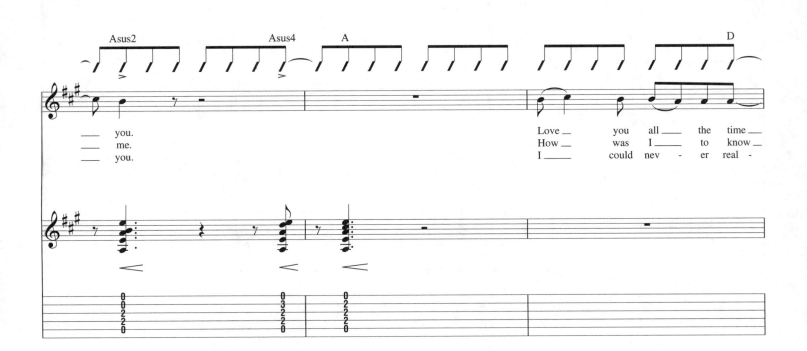

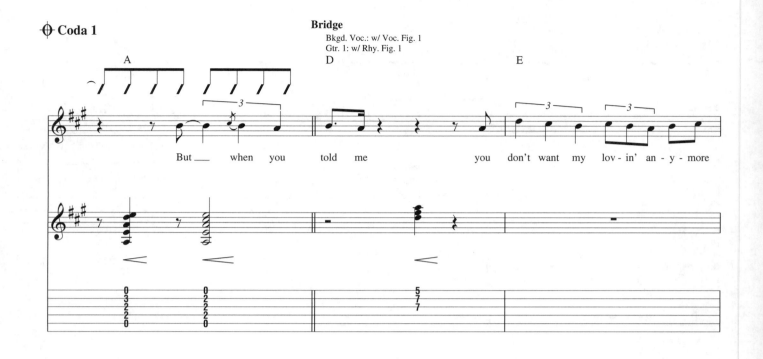

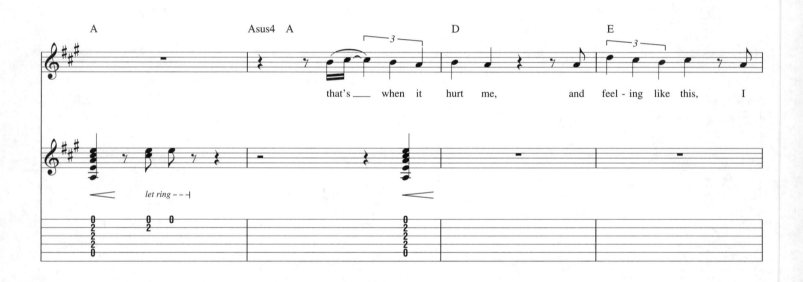

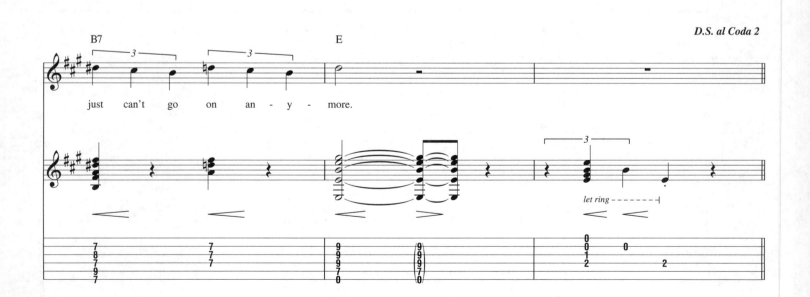

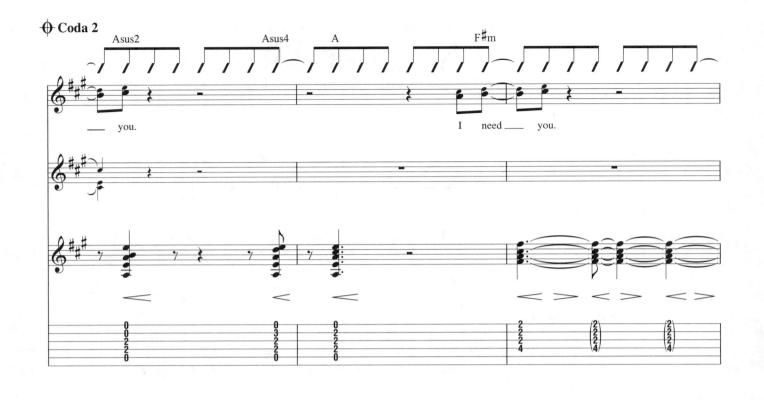

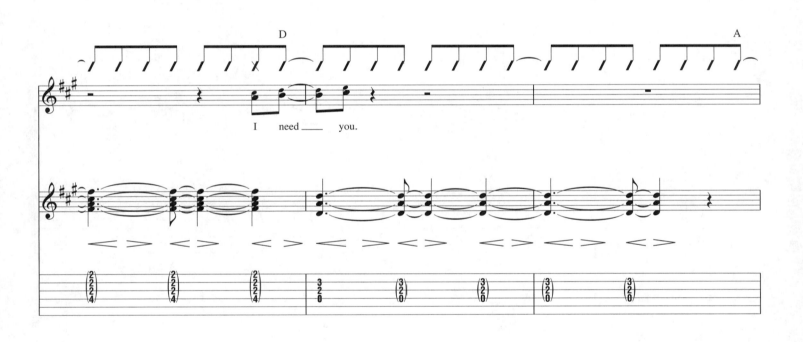

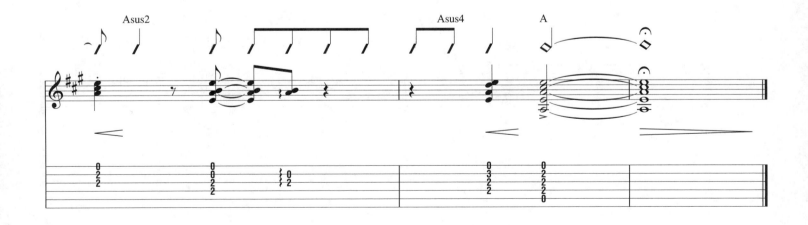

from *Help!* Original Motion Picture Soundtrack

Another Girl

Words and Music by John Lennon and Paul McCartney

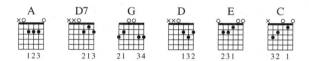

* Recording sounds 1/4 step flat.

§ Verse

2nd time, Gtr. 2: w/ Fill 1

an - oth - er girl. _____ 1. You're mak - ing me say _____ that I've _____ got
3. I don't _____ want to say _____ that I've _____ been

no - bod - y but you. _____ But as _____ from to - day, well, I've _____ got
un - hap - py with you. _____ But as _____ from to - day, well, I've _____ seen

Gtr. 2 tacet

2nd time, Gtr. 2: w/ Fill 2

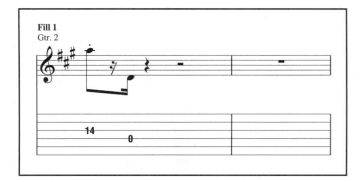

Fill 1
Gtr. 2

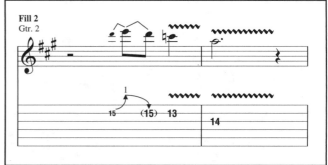

Fill 2
Gtr. 2

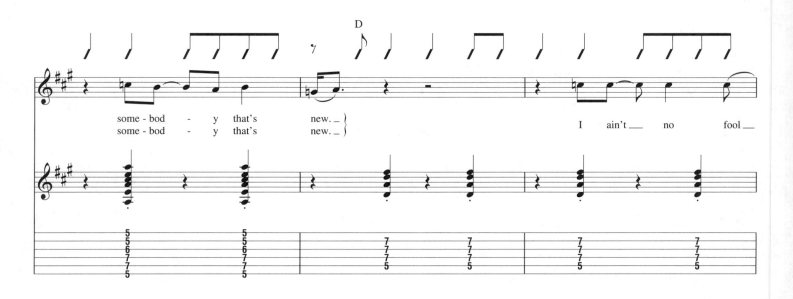

some - bod - y that's new. _
some - bod - y that's new. _

I ain't __ no fool __

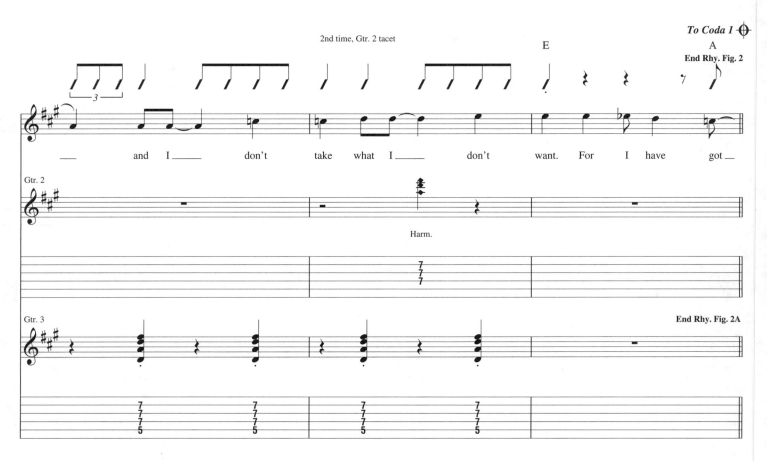

2nd time, Gtr. 2 tacet

__ and I __ don't take what I __ don't want. For I have got __

Gtr. 2

Harm.

Gtr. 3

To Coda 1 ⊕

End Rhy. Fig. 2

End Rhy. Fig. 2A

Chorus

Gtrs. 1 & 3: w/ Rhy. Figs. 1 & 1A

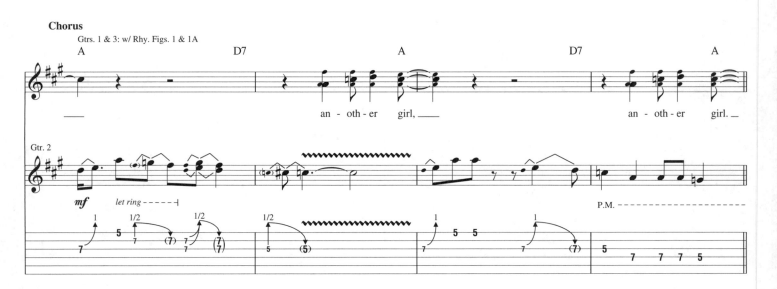

an - oth - er girl, __

an - oth - er girl.

Gtr. 2

mf   *let ring - - - - -*

P.M. - - - - - - - - - - - - - - - - - -

Coda 2

Verse

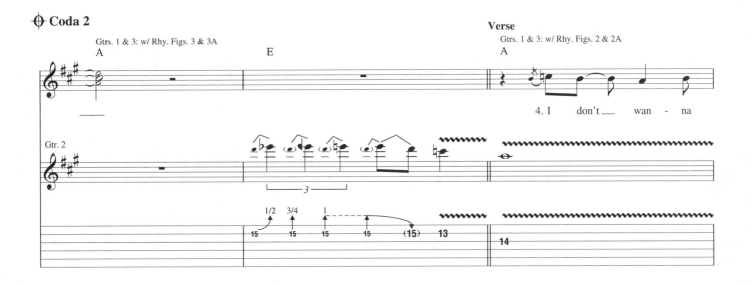

Gtrs. 1 & 3: w/ Rhy. Figs. 3 & 3A

Gtrs. 1 & 3: w/ Rhy. Figs. 2 & 2A

4. I don't wan-na

say that I've been un-hap-py with you.

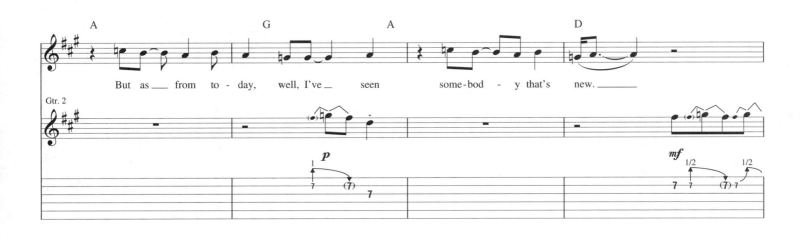

But as from to-day, well, I've seen some-bod-y that's new.

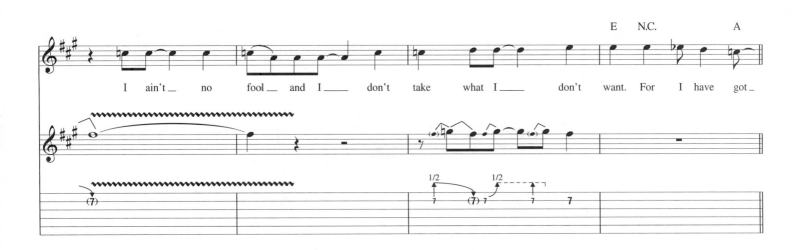

I ain't no fool and I don't take what I don't want. For I have got

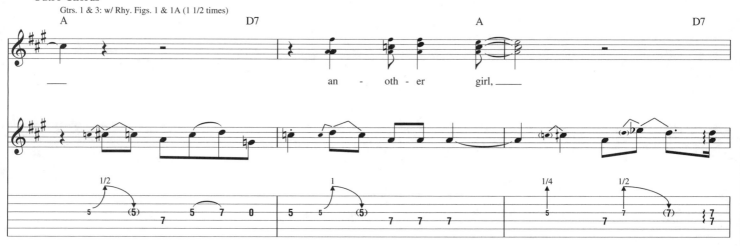

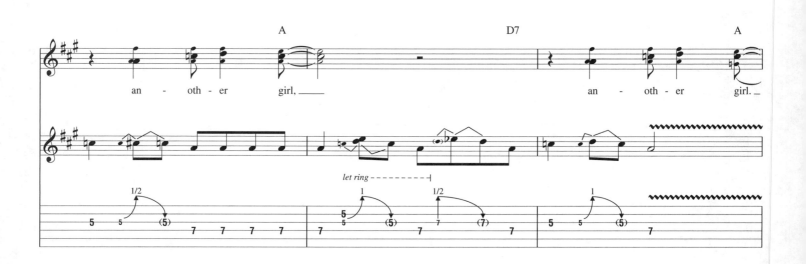

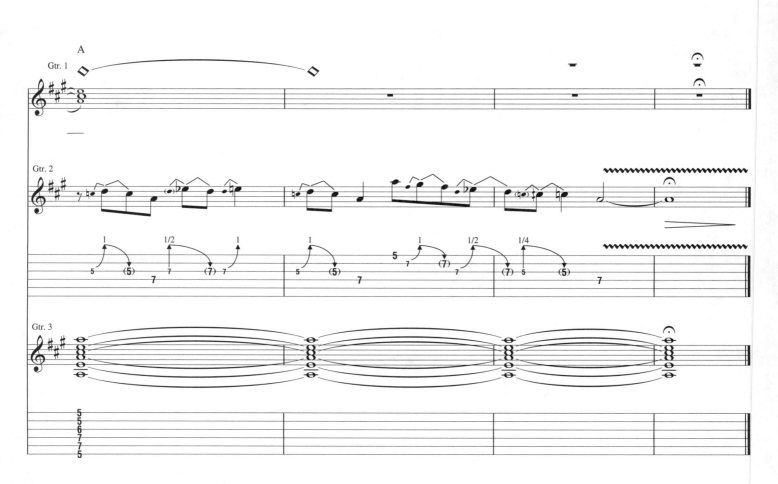

Another Hard Day's Night

Words and Music by John Lennon and Paul McCartney

Open G tuning, capo V:
(low to high) D–G–D–G–B–D

*Sitar arr. for gtr.

**Symbols in parentheses represent chord names respective to capoed guitars.
Symbols above reflect actual sounding chords. Capoed fret is "0" in tab.
Chord symbols reflect basic harmony.
***Let lower open strings ring throughout. Staccato applies to top 'melody' notes only.

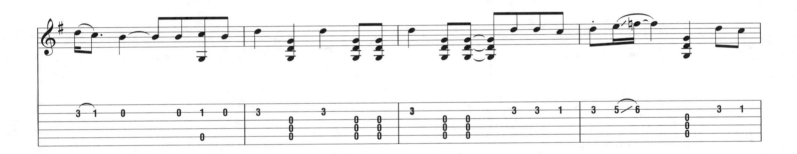

*Sitar arr. for gtr.

from *Help!* Original Motion Picture Soundtrack

Ticket to Ride

Words and Music by John Lennon and Paul McCartney

*Chord symbols reflect implied harmony.

**See top of page for chord diagrams pertaining to rhythm slashes.

⊕ Coda

Outro
Double-time feel

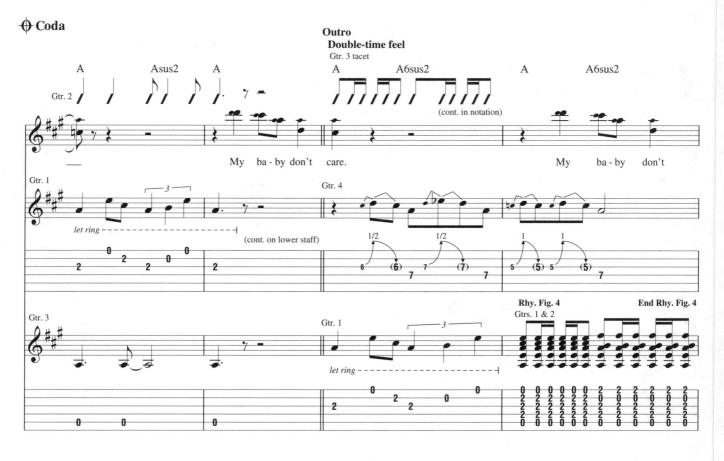

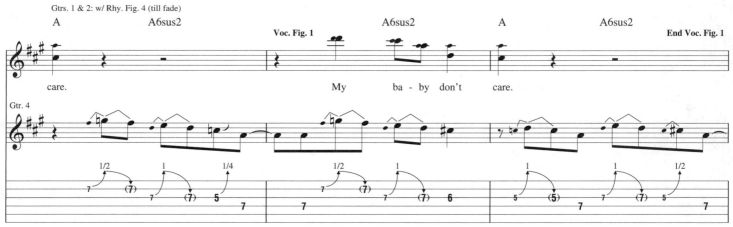

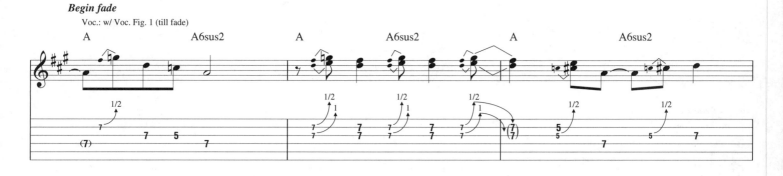

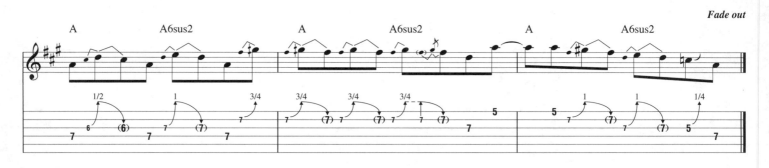

The Bitter End/You Can't Do That

THE BITTER END
By Kenneth Thorne
Free time

*Strings arr. for gtr.

**Harp arr. for gtr.

***Glockenspiel arr. for gtr.

†Strings arr. for gtr.

172

YOU CAN'T DO THAT
Words and Music by John Lennon and Paul McCartney

Gtr. 2: Baritone gtr. tuning:
(low to high:) G-C-F-B♭-D-G

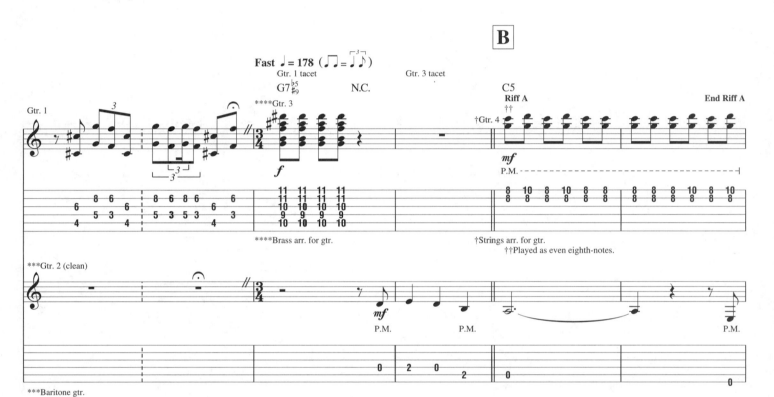

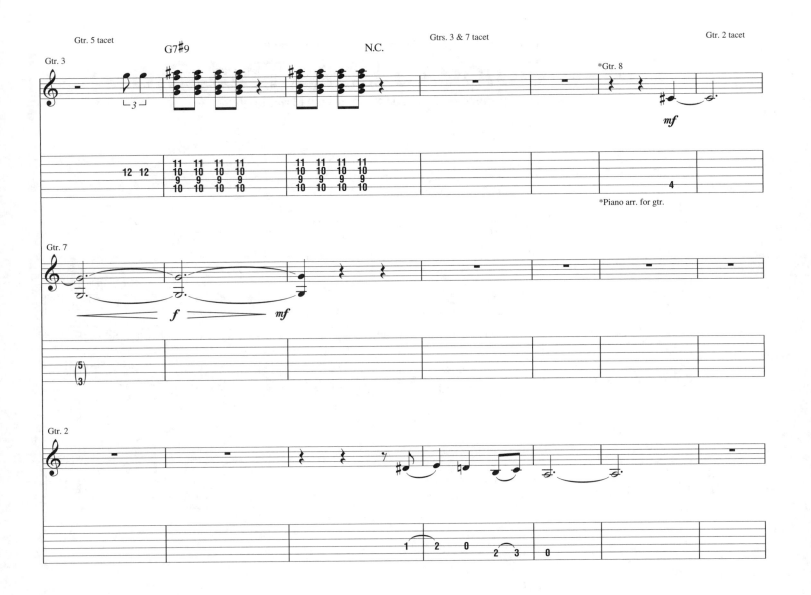

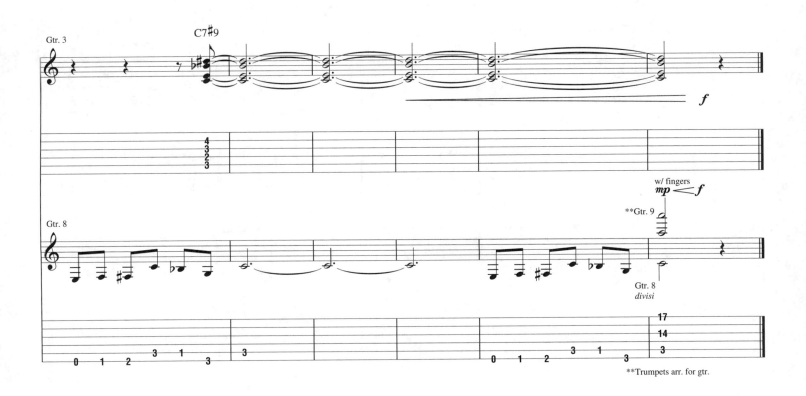

You're Going to Lose That Girl

Words and Music by John Lennon and Paul McCartney

*Piano arr. for gtr.   **Chord symbols reflect basic harmony.

girl.＿   girl,＿   you're gon-na   lose.＿＿＿＿＿

(Yes,   yes, you're gon-na   lose that   girl.)＿

Bridge

I'll make a point   of tak-ing her a-way from   you,＿＿＿

(Watch   what you＿ do.)＿

from *Rubber Soul*

I've Just Seen a Face
Words and Music by John Lennon and Paul McCartney

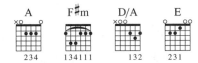

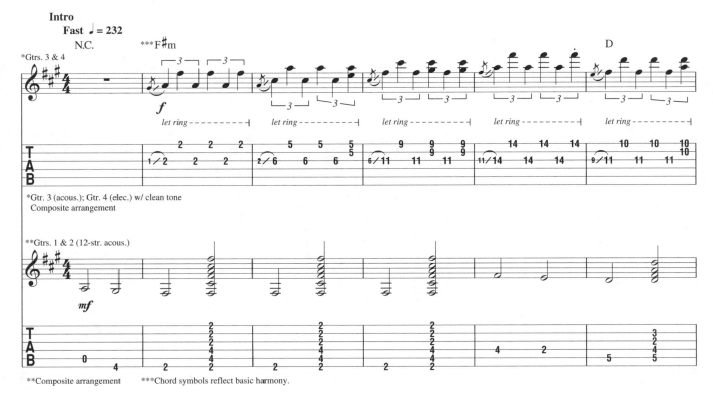

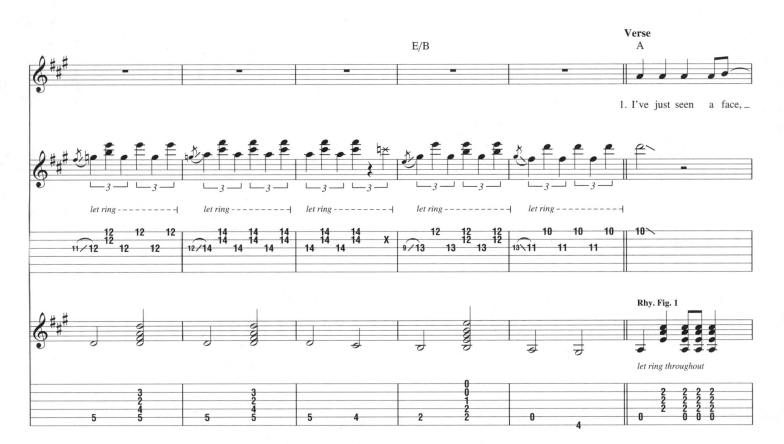

182

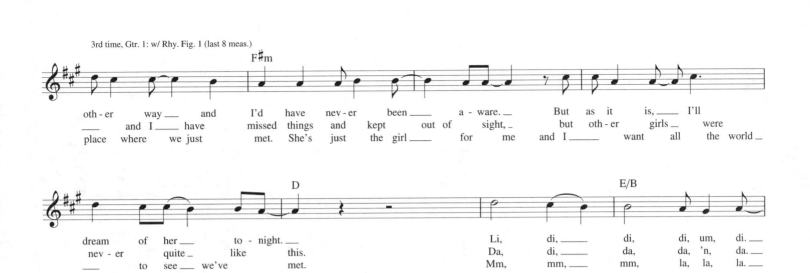

3rd time, Gtr. 1: w/ Rhy. Fig. 1 (last 8 meas.)

F#m

oth- er way ___ and I'd have nev- er been ___ a- ware. ___ But as it is, ___ I'll
___ and I ___ have missed things and kept out of sight, ___ but oth- er girls ___ were
place where we just met. She's just the girl ___ for me and I ___ want all the world ___

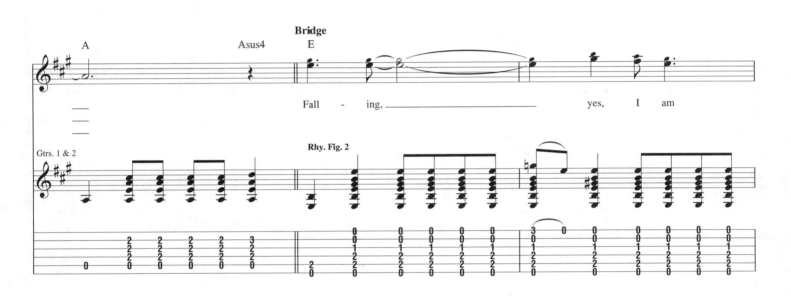

D

E/B

dream of her ___ to- night. ___ Li, di, ___ di, di, um, di.
nev- er quite ___ like this. Da, di, ___ da, da, 'n, da.
___ to see ___ we've met. Mm, mm, ___ mm, la, la, la. ___

A   Asus4   **Bridge**
                          E

Fall - ing, _____ yes, I am

Gtrs. 1 & 2   **Rhy. Fig. 2**

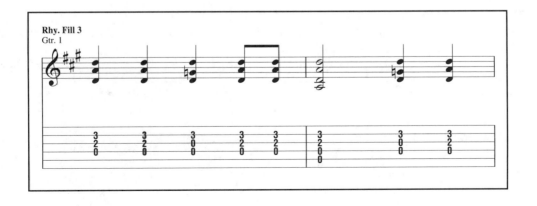

3rd time, Gtr. 1: w/ Rhy. Fill 3

D/A   A

fall - ing, ___   and she keeps call - ing ___

Rhy. Fill 3
Gtr. 1

183

Bridge

Gtrs. 1 & 2: w/ Rhy. Fig. 2
Gtr. 5 tacet

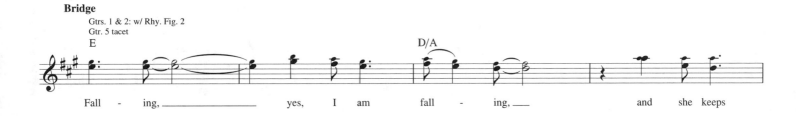

Fall - ing, _____ yes, I am fall - ing, _____ and she keeps

D.S al Coda

Gtrs. 1 & 2: w/ Rhy. Fill 1

call - ing _____ me back _____ a - gain. _____

⊕ Coda

Fall - ing, _____ yes, I am

fall - ing, _____ and she keeps call - ing _____

185

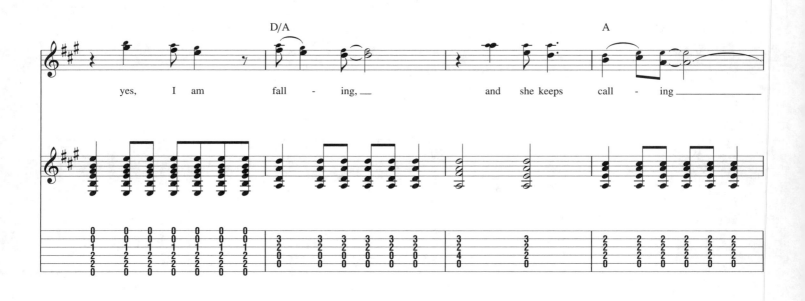

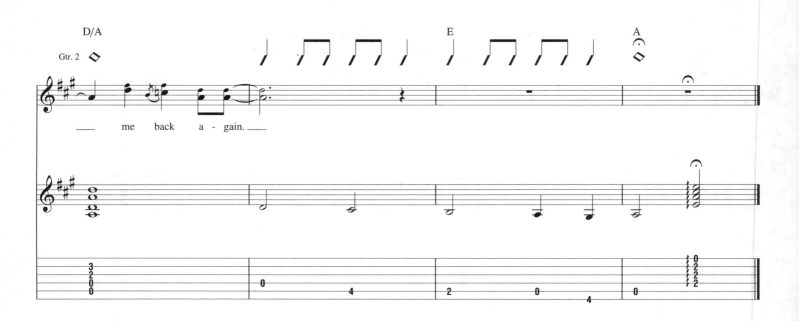

from *Rubber Soul*

Norwegian Wood
(This Bird Has Flown)

Words and Music by John Lennon and Paul McCartney

Gtrs. 1, 2 & 3: Capo II
Gtr. 4: Capo VII

Intro

Moderately ♩. = 60

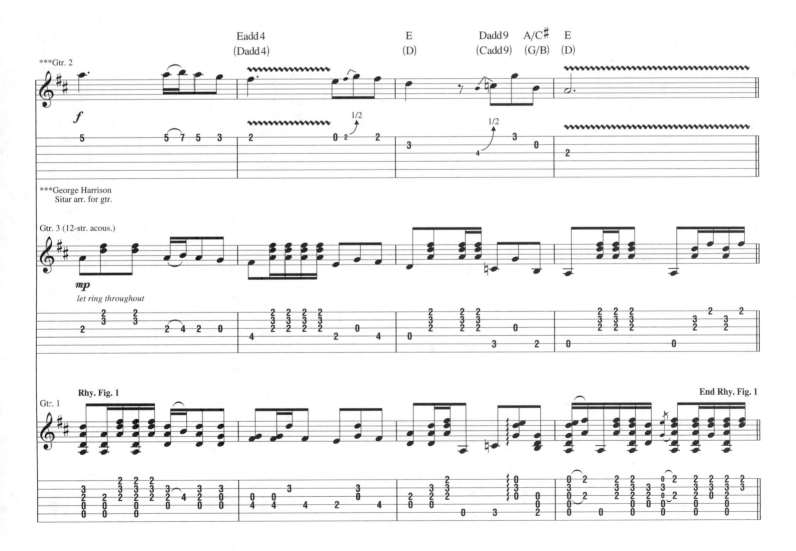

*John Lennon

**Symbols in parentheses represent chord names respective to capoed guitars.
Symbols above reflect actual sounding chords. Capoed fret is "0" in tab.
Chord symbols reflect basic harmony.

***George Harrison
Sitar arr. for gtr.

Verse

John Lennon:

1. I once had a girl, ___ or should I say she once had me.

She showed me her room, is-n't it good, Nor-we-gian wood. She

Rhy. Fig. 2A

Rhy. Fig. 2

End Rhy. Fig. 2A

End Rhy. Fig. 2

*Symbols in double parentheses represent chord names respective to capoed Gtr. 4.

**Paul McCartney, harmony vocals

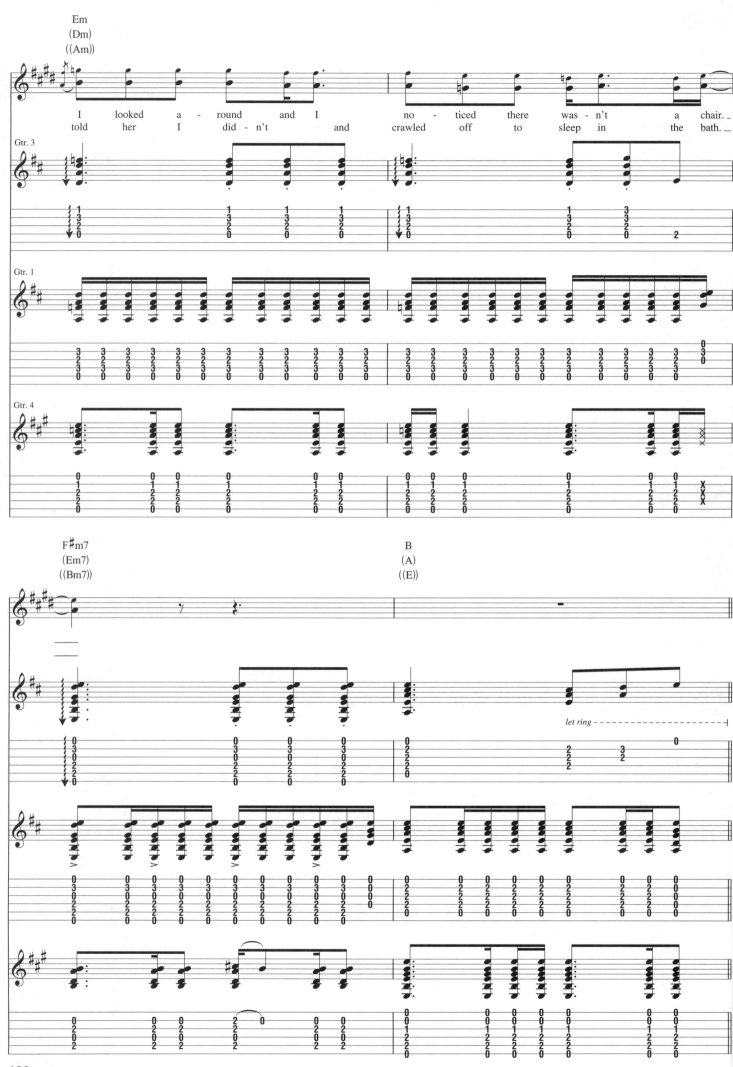

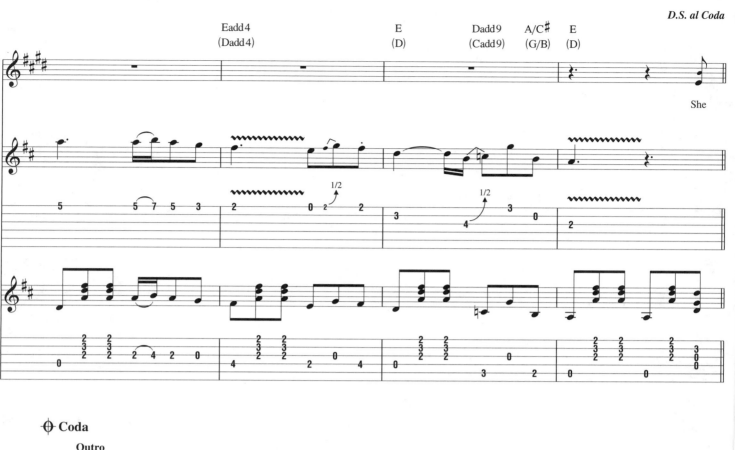

She

Coda

Outro

from *Rubber Soul*

You Won't See Me

Words and Music by John Lennon and Paul McCartney

*Piano arr. for gtr.

**Chord symbols reflect basic harmony.

your age. ____ We have lost ____ the time ____ that

was so hard ____ to find. ____ And I ____ will lose my mind ____ if

you won't ___ see me. ___ You won't ___ see me. ___ 2. I don't know ___

(You won't see me. You won't see me.)

End Rhy. Fig. 1

End Rhy. Fig. 1A

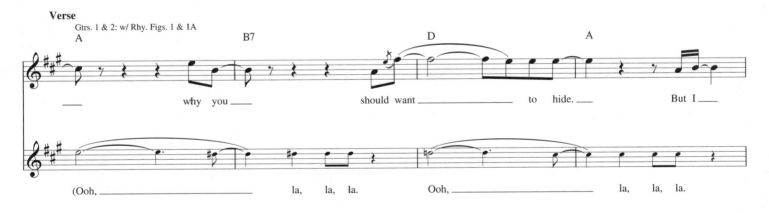

Verse

Gtrs. 1 & 2: w/ Rhy. Figs. 1 & 1A

| A | B7 | D | A |

___ why you ___ should want ___ to hide. ___ But I ___

(Ooh, ___ la, la, la. Ooh, ___ la, la, la.

| B7 | D | A |

can't get through, ___ my hands ___ are tied. ___ I won't want ___

Ooh, ___ la, la, la. Ooh, ___ la, la, la.

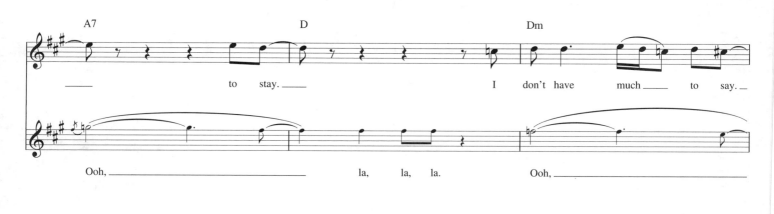

to stay. I don't have much to say.

Ooh, la, la, la. Ooh,

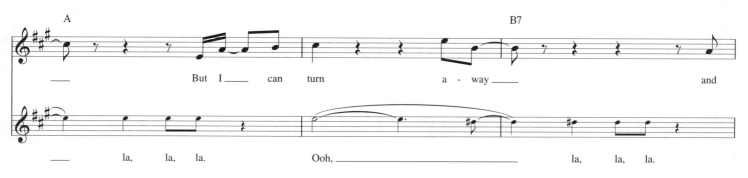

But I can turn a - way and

la, la, la. Ooh, la, la, la.

you won't see me. You won't see me.

You won't see me. You won't see me.)

Bridge

Time af - ter time you re - fuse to e - ven lis - ten.

Gtr. 1

Gtr. 2

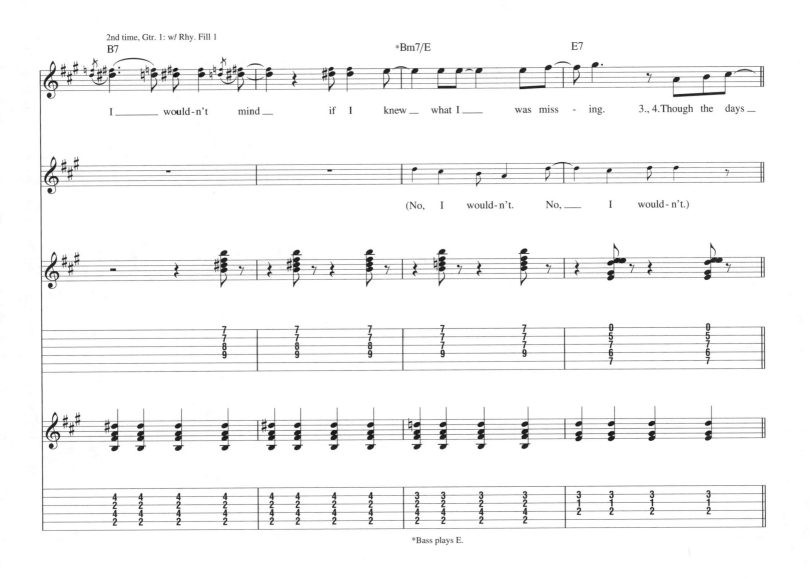

I _____ would-n't mind _____ if I knew _____ what I _____ was miss - ing. 3., 4.Though the days _____

(No, I would-n't. No, _____ I would-n't.)

*Bass plays E.

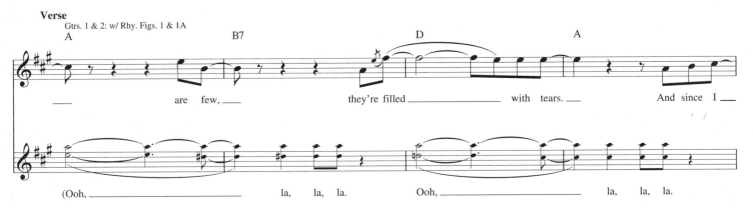

Verse

_____ are few, _____ they're filled _____ with tears. _____ And since I _____

(Ooh, _____ la, la, la. Ooh, _____ la, la, la.

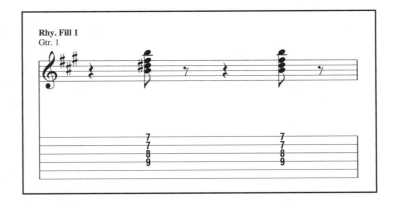

Rhy. Fill 1
Gtr. 1

lost you, _____ it feels _____ like years. _____ Yes, it seems _____

Ooh, _____ la, la, la. Ooh, _____ la, la, la.

_____ so long, _____ girl, since you've _____ been gone _____

Ooh, _____ la, la, la. Ooh, _____

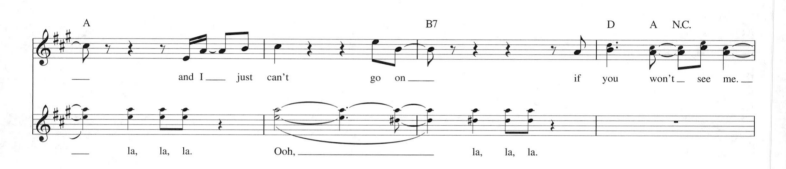

_____ and I _____ just can't go on _____ if you won't _____ see me. _____

_____ la, la, la. Ooh, _____ la, la, la.

_____ You won't _____ see me. _____ _____ Yeah. _____

You won't _____ see me. You won't _____ see me.) You won't _____ see me.)

Outro
Gtrs. 1 & 2: w/ Rhy. Figs. 1 & 1A (till fade)

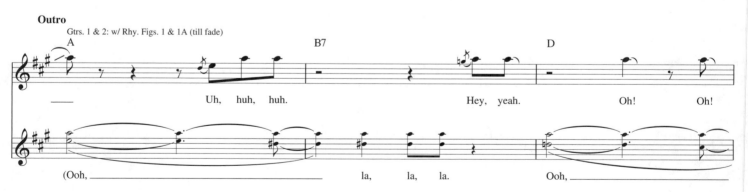

_____ Uh, huh, huh. Hey, yeah. Oh! Oh!

(Ooh, _____ la, la, la. Ooh, _____

Begin Fade   *Fade out*

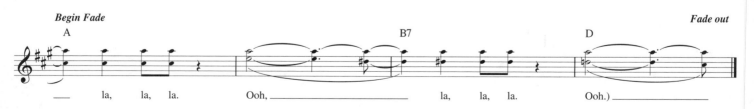

_____ la, la, la. Ooh, _____ la, la, la. Ooh.)

Think for Yourself

Words and Music by George Harrison

Gtr. 1: Capo III

*Bass arr. for gtr. **Symbols in parentheses represent chord names respective to capoed guitar.
Symbols above reflect actual sounding chords. Capoed fret is "0" in tab.

Chorus

Do what you want to do ___ and go where you're go-ing to. ___

Think for your-self 'cause I ___ won't be there with you. ___

Fill 3
Gtr. 2

Fill 4
Gtr. 2

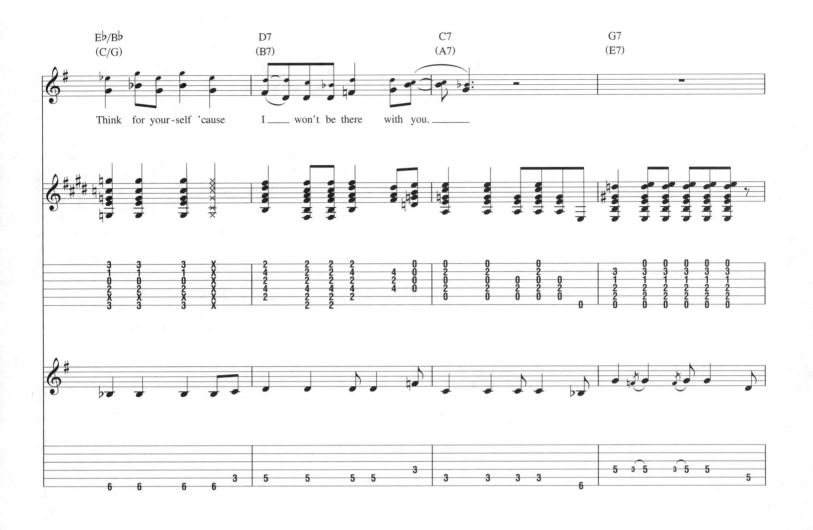

Think for your-self 'cause I ___ won't be there with you. ___

Think for your-self 'cause I ___ won't be there with you. ___

from *Rubber Soul*

The Word

Words and Music by John Lennon and Paul McCartney

Intro
Moderately ♩ = 126

1. Say the

*Gtr. 1
*Piano arr. for gtr.
Gtr. 2 (clean)

**Chord symbols reflects overall harmony.

Chorus

D7#9

2nd time, Gtr. 2: w/ Rhy. Fill 1

(1., 3.) word _____ and you'll be free.   Say the word _____ and be like me.   Say the
(2.) word _____ and you'll be free.   Spread the word _____ and be like me.   Spread the

Rhy. Fig. 1

Rhy. Fig. 1A

Rhy. Fill 1
Gtr. 2

word _____ I'm think - ing of. Have you heard? _____ The word _ is "love." It's

so fine, _ it's sun - shine. _ It's the word _____ "love." _

End Rhy. Fig. 1

End Rhy. Fig. 1A

Verse

1. In the be-gin-ning I mis-un-der-stood, but now I've got it, the
2. Ev-'ry-where I go I hear it said, in the good and the bad books that
3. Now that I know what I feel must be right, I'm here to show ev-'ry-

1., 2. 2nd time, Gtr. 2: w/ Fill 1

3.

word is good. 2. Spread the bod - y the light. 4. Give the
I have read. 3. Say the

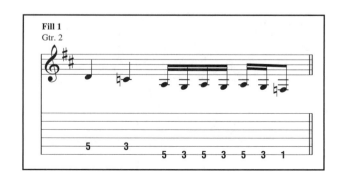

Fill 1
Gtr. 2

from *Rubber Soul*

Michelle

Words and Music by John Lennon and Paul McCartney

*Symbols in parentheses represent chord names respective to capoed guitars.
Symbols above reflect actual sounding chords. Capoed fret is "0" in tab.

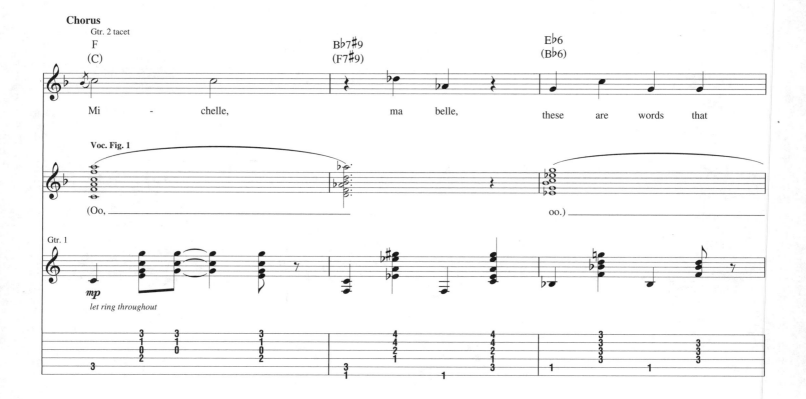

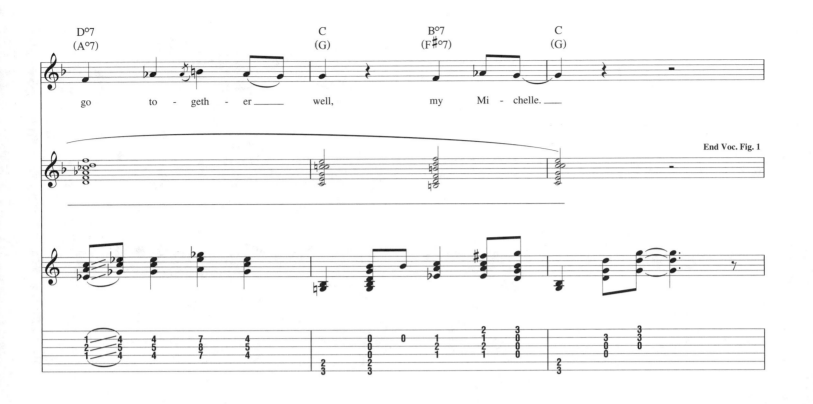

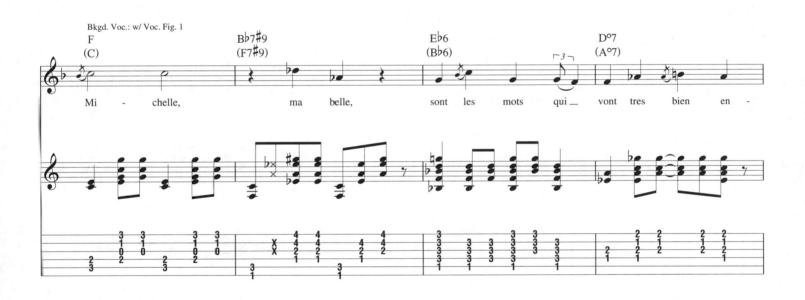

that's all I ___ want to say.   Un - til I   find   a   way, _____   I will

(Oo, _____   oo.)

say   the   on - ly   words   I   know   that   you'll   un - der - stand.

Chorus

Mi - chelle,   ma   belle,   sont   les   mots   qui ___ vont   tres   bien   en - semble, ___

from *Rubber Soul*

It's Only Love

Words and Music by John Lennon and Paul McCartney

*Symbols in parentheses represent chord names respective to capoed guitars.
Symbols above represent actual sounding chords. Capoed fret is "0" in tab.
Chord symbols reflect basic harmony.

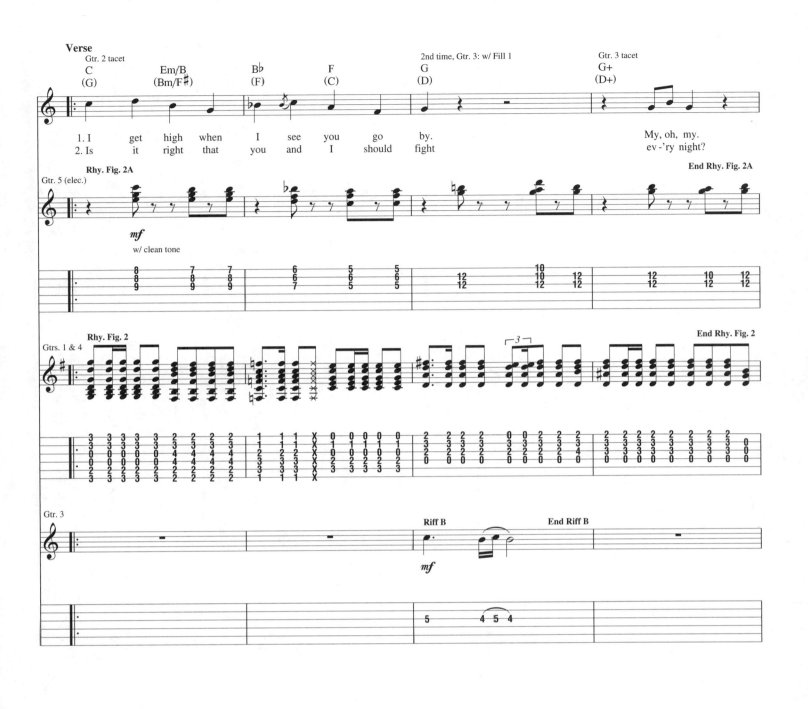

Gtr. 2 tacet

2nd time, Gtr. 3: w/ Fill 1

Gtr. 3 tacet

C (G) Em/B (Bm/F#) B♭ (F) F (C) G (D) G+ (D+)

1. I get high when I see you go by. My, oh, my.
2. Is it right that you and I should fight ev-'ry night?

Rhy. Fig. 2A **End Rhy. Fig. 2A**

Gtr. 5 (elec.)

mf

w/ clean tone

Rhy. Fig. 2 **End Rhy. Fig. 2**

Gtrs. 1 & 4

Gtr. 3

Riff B **End Riff B**

mf

Gtrs. 1 & 4: w/ Rhy. Fig. 2
Gtr. 5: w/ Rhy. Fig. 2A

1st time, Gtr. 3: w/ Riff B
2nd time, Gtr. 3: w/ Fill 2

C (G) Em/B (Bm/F#) B♭ (F) F (C) G (D) G+ (D+)

When you sigh, my mind in - side just flies, but - ter - flies. __
Just the sight of you makes night time bright, ver - y bright. __

Fill 1

Gtr. 3

Fill 2

Gtr. 3

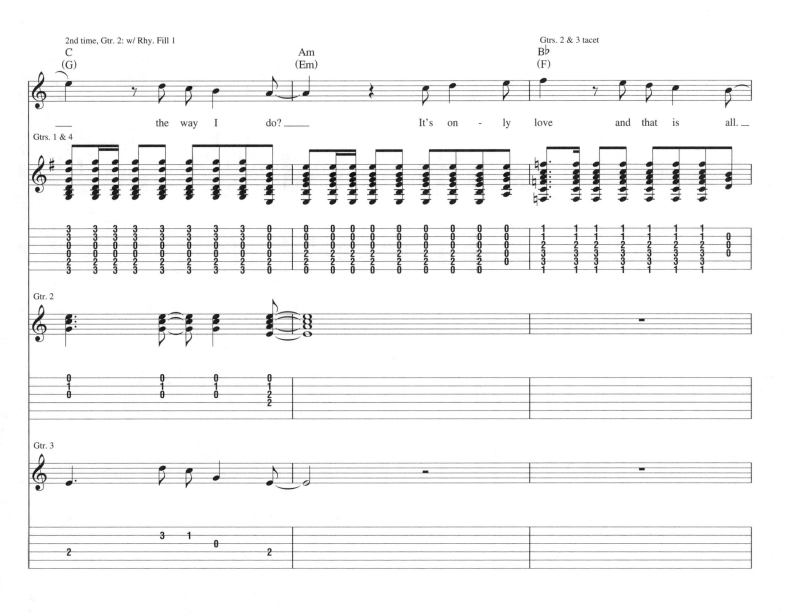

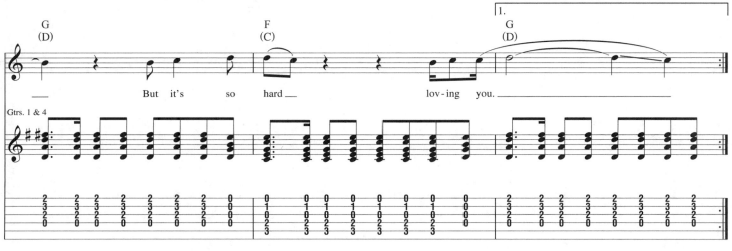

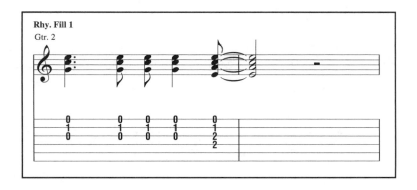

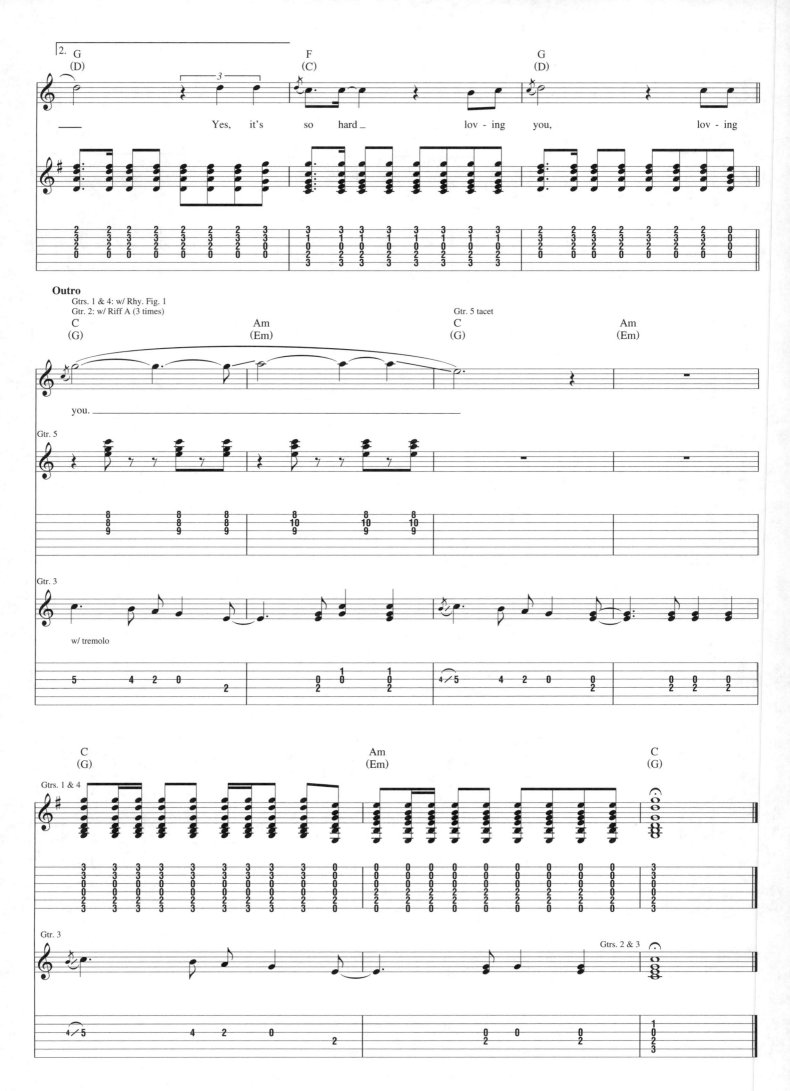

Girl

Words and Music by John Lennon and Paul McCartney

*Symbols in parentheses represent chord names respective to capoed guitars.
Symbols above reflect actual sounding chords. Capoed fret is "0" in tab.
Chord symbols reflect basic harmony.

** Bass plays C.

***Sung behind the beat.

†Sung as even eighth-notes.

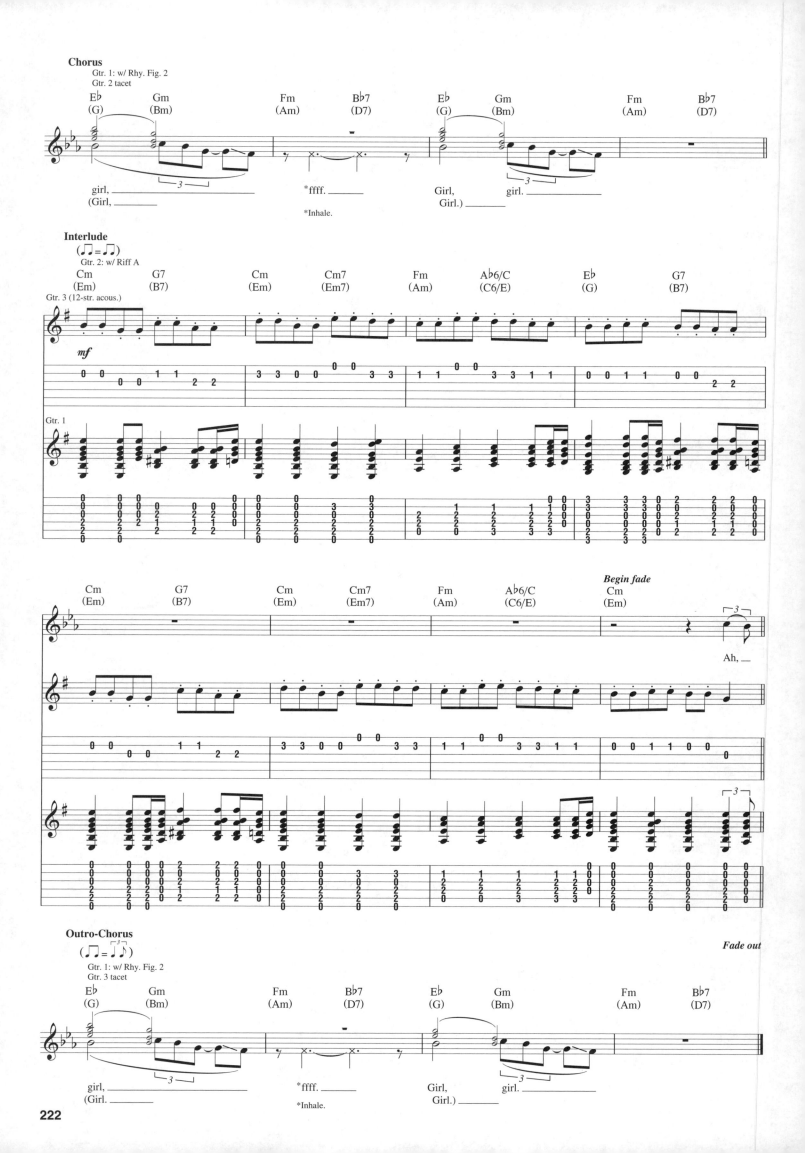

222

from *Rubber Soul*

I'm Looking Through You

Words and Music by John Lennon and Paul McCartney

Capo I

Intro

Moderately fast ♩ = 168

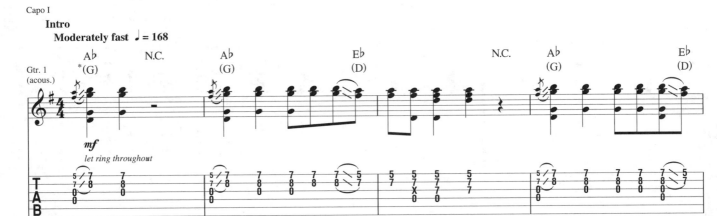

*Symbols in parentheses represent chord names respective to capoed guitar.
Symbols above reflect actual sounding chords. Capoed fret is "0" in tab.
Chord symbols reflect basic harmony.

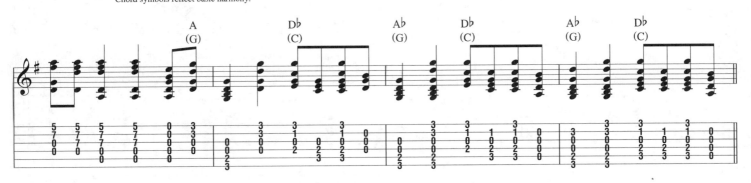

Verse

2nd time, Gtr. 2: w/ Fill 1

1. I'm look-ing through you, where did you go?
2. Your lips are mov-ing, I can-not

Fill 1
Gtr. 2

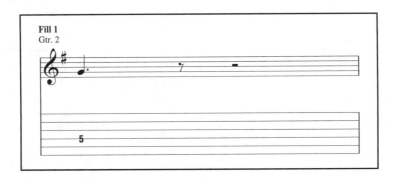

224

𝄋 Bridge

2nd time, Gtr. 2 tacet

2nd time, Gtr. 2: w/ Fill 3

Why, — tell me why — did you — not treat me right? —

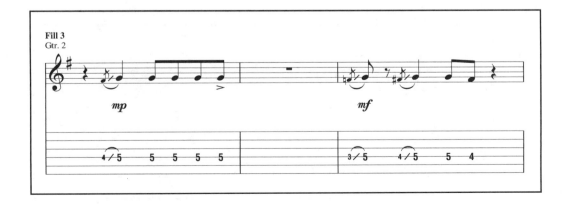

Fill 3
Gtr. 2

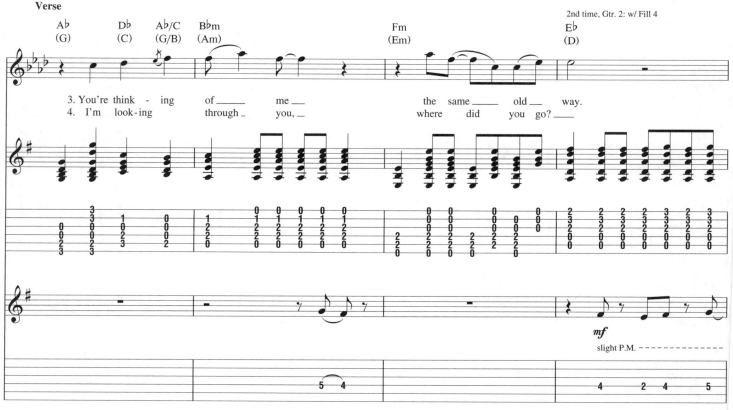

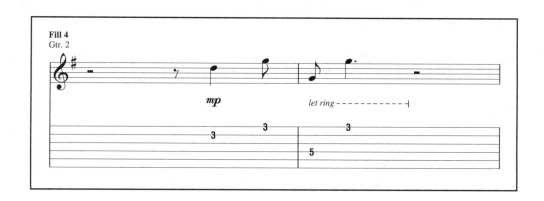

from *Rubber Soul*

In My Life

Words and Music by John Lennon and Paul McCartney

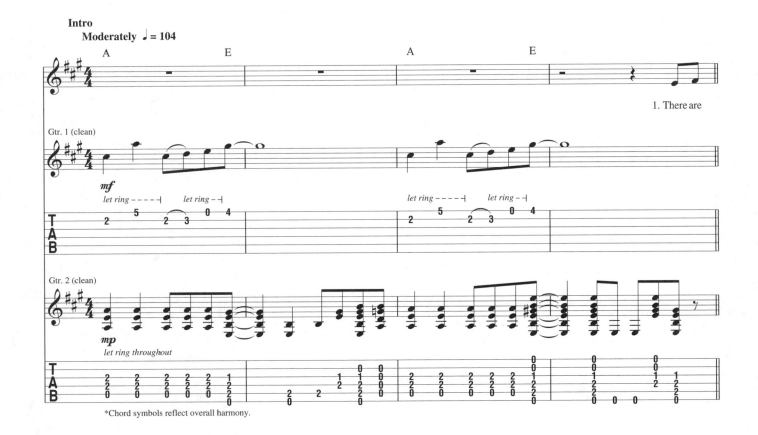

*Chord symbols reflect overall harmony.

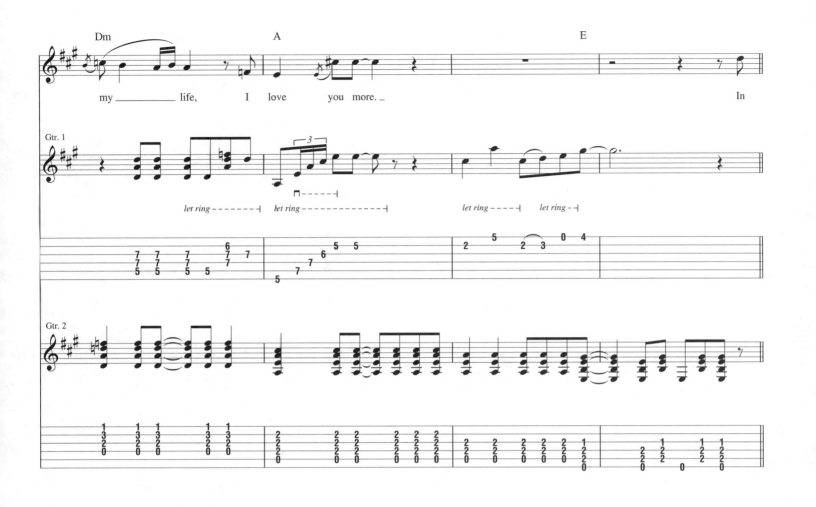

my _____ life, I love you more. In

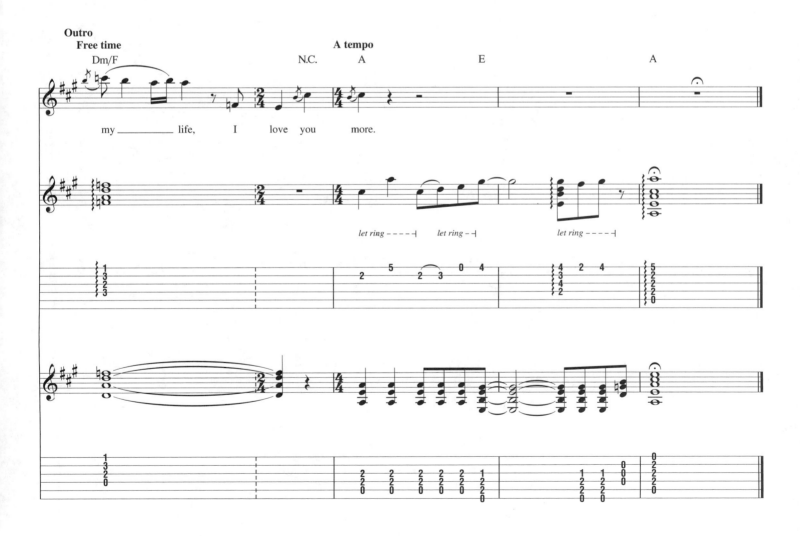

my _____ life, I love you more.

from *Rubber Soul*

Wait

Words and Music by John Lennon and Paul McCartney

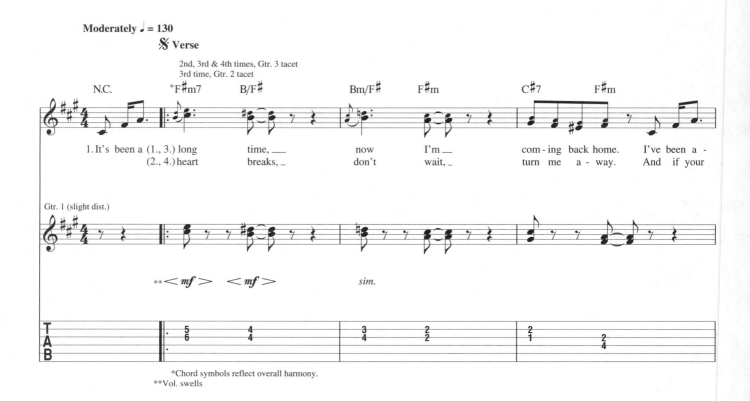

*Chord symbols reflect overall harmony.
**Vol. swells

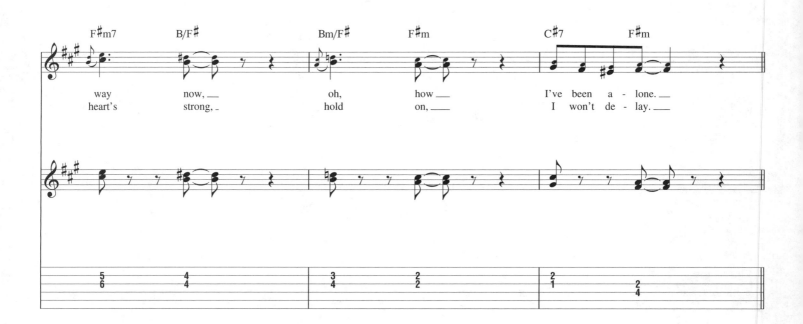

Chorus

2nd, 3rd & 4th times, Gtr. 1: w/ Rhy. Fill 1

Wait till I come back _ to your side. _____ We for -

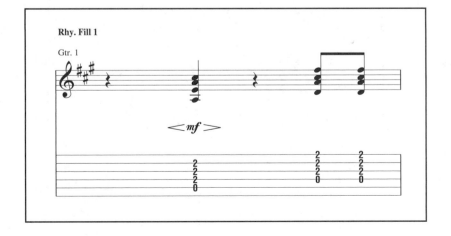

*Sung behind the beat.

Coda 1

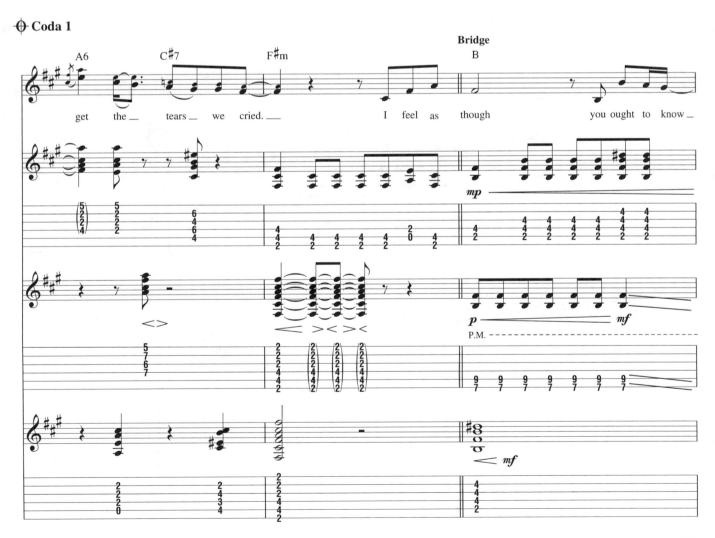

Coda 2

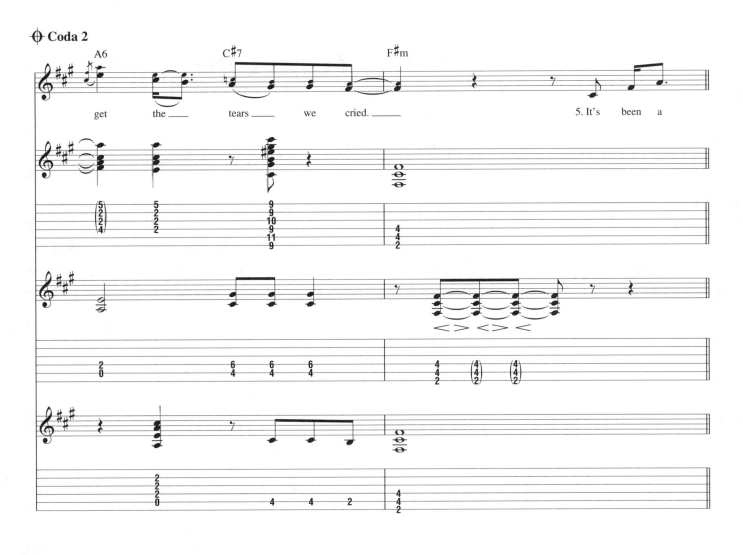

get the ___ tears ___ we cried. ___

5. It's been a

Verse

Gtrs. 2 & 3 tacet

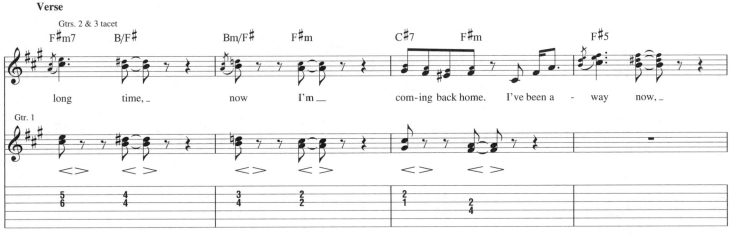

long time, ___ now I'm ___ com-ing back home. I've been a - way now, ___

Gtr. 1

oh, how ___ I've been a - lone.

Gtrs. 1 & 3

Run for Your Life

Words and Music by John Lennon and Paul McCartney

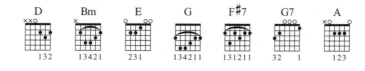

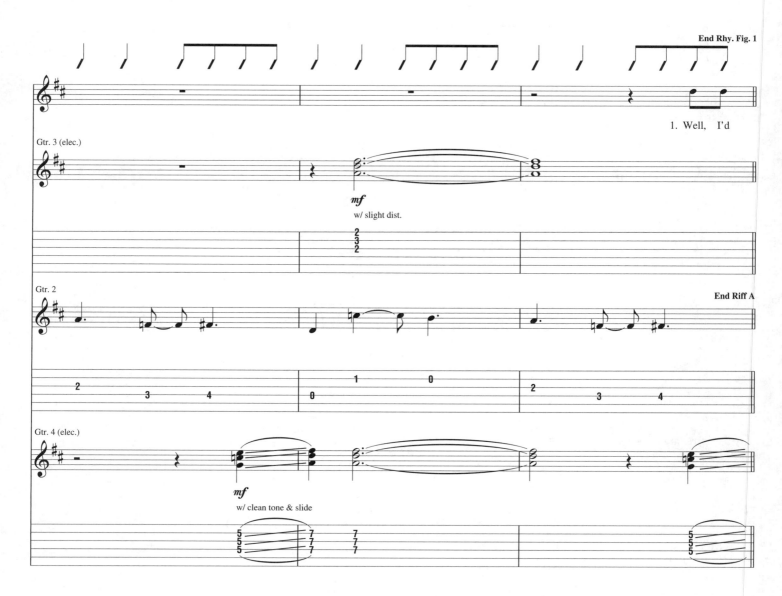

Catch you with an - oth - er man, ___ that's the end, ___ ah, lit - tle girl.

w/out slide

Interlude

Gtr. 1: w/ Rhy. Fig. 1
Gtr. 2: w/ Riff A
Gtr. 3 tacet

D

2. Well, you
4. I'd

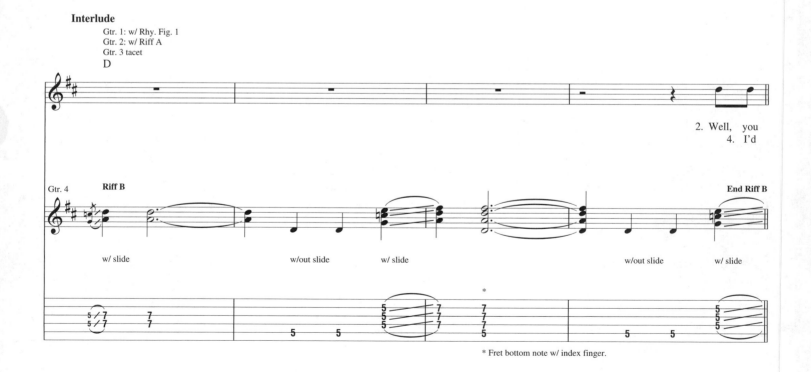

w/ slide   w/out slide   w/ slide   w/out slide   w/ slide

* Fret bottom note w/ index finger.

Verse

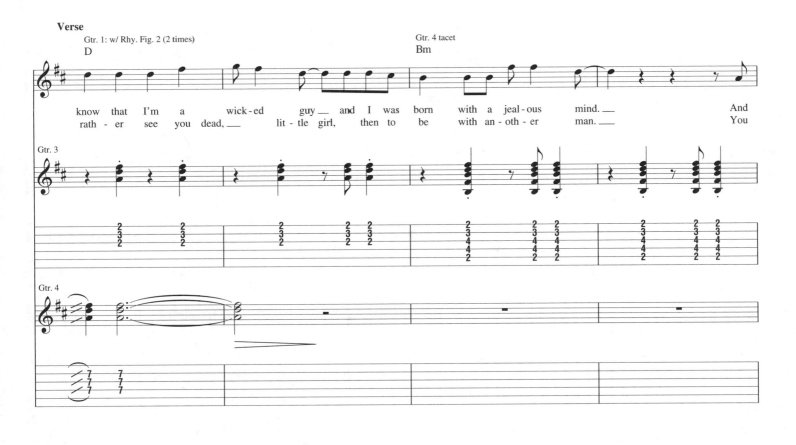

Chorus

To Coda ⊕

Guitar Notation Legend

Guitar music can be notated three different ways: on a *musical staff*, in *tablature*, and in *rhythm slashes*.

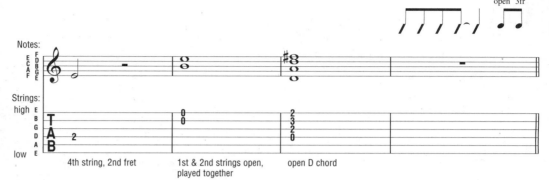

RHYTHM SLASHES are written above the staff. Strum chords in the rhythm indicated. Use the chord diagrams found at the top of the first page of the transcription for the appropriate chord voicings. Round noteheads indicate single notes.

THE MUSICAL STAFF shows pitches and rhythms and is divided by bar lines into measures. Pitches are named after the first seven letters of the alphabet.

TABLATURE graphically represents the guitar fingerboard. Each horizontal line represents a string, and each number represents a fret.

4th string, 2nd fret

1st & 2nd strings open, played together

open D chord

HALF-STEP BEND: Strike the note and bend up 1/2 step.

WHOLE-STEP BEND: Strike the note and bend up one step.

GRACE NOTE BEND: Strike the note and immediately bend up as indicated.

SLIGHT (MICROTONE) BEND: Strike the note and bend up 1/4 step.

BEND AND RELEASE: Strike the note and bend up as indicated, then release back to the original note. Only the first note is struck.

PRE-BEND: Bend the note as indicated, then strike it.

VIBRATO: The string is vibrated by rapidly bending and releasing the note with the fretting hand.

WIDE VIBRATO: The pitch is varied to a greater degree by vibrating with the fretting hand.

HAMMER-ON: Strike the first (lower) note with one finger, then sound the higher note (on the same string) with another finger by fretting it without picking.

PULL-OFF: Place both fingers on the notes to be sounded. Strike the first note and without picking, pull the finger off to sound the second (lower) note.

LEGATO SLIDE: Strike the first note and then slide the same fret-hand finger up or down to the second note. The second note is not struck.

SHIFT SLIDE: Same as legato slide, except the second note is struck.

TRILL: Very rapidly alternate between the notes indicated by continuously hammering on and pulling off.

TAPPING: Hammer ("tap") the fret indicated with the pick-hand index or middle finger and pull off to the note fretted by the fret hand.

NATURAL HARMONIC: Strike the note while the fret-hand lightly touches the string directly over the fret indicated.

PINCH HARMONIC: The note is fretted normally and a harmonic is produced by adding the edge of the thumb or the tip of the index finger of the pick hand to the normal pick attack.

PICK SCRAPE: The edge of the pick is rubbed down (or up) the string, producing a scratchy sound.

MUFFLED STRINGS: A percussive sound is produced by laying the fret hand across the string(s) without depressing, and striking them with the pick hand.

PALM MUTING: The note is partially muted by the pick hand lightly touching the string(s) just before the bridge.

RAKE: Drag the pick across the strings indicated with a single motion.

TREMOLO PICKING: The note is picked as rapidly and continuously as possible.

VIBRATO BAR DIVE AND RETURN: The pitch of the note or chord is dropped a specified number of steps (in rhythm), then returned to the original pitch.

VIBRATO BAR SCOOP: Depress the bar just before striking the note, then quickly release the bar.

VIBRATO BAR DIP: Strike the note and then immediately drop a specified number of steps, then release back to the original pitch.